SISKIYOU COUNTY LIBRARY

D0192126

FinancialRelief
FOR SINGLE PARENTS

OFFICIALLY
DISCARDED

Generously donated by
Siskiyou/Modoc Child
Support Services

2008

OFFICIALLY
DISCARDED

FinancialRelief
FOR SINGLE PARENTS

A Proven Plan for Achieving the Seemingly Impossible

332.024
786

Brenda Armstrong
ııı

Moody Publishers
CHICAGO

SISKIYOU COUNTY PUBLIC LIBRARY
719 FOURTH STREET
YREKA, CALIFORNIA 96097

© 2007 by
BRENDA ARMSTRONG

All rights reserved. No part of this book may be reproduced in any form without permission in writing from the publisher, except in the case of brief quotations embodied in critical articles or reviews.

All Scripture quotations, unless otherwise indicated, are taken from the *Holy Bible, New International Version®. NIV®.* Copyright © 1973, 1978, 1984 by International Bible Society. Used by permission of Zondervan. All rights reserved.

Scripture quotations marked NASB are taken from the *New American Standard Bible®,* Copyright © 1960, 1962, 1963, 1968, 1971, 1972, 1973, 1975, 1977, 1995 by The Lockman Foundation. Used by permission. (www.Lockman.org)

Scripture quotations marked NLT are taken from the *Holy Bible, New Living Translation,* copyright © 1996. Used by permission of Tyndale House Publishers, Inc., Wheaton, Illinois 60189, U.S.A. All rights reserved.

Scripture quotations marked TNIV are taken from the *Holy Bible, Today's New International Version* TNIV®. Copyright© 2001, 2005 by International Bible Society. Used by permission of Zondervan. All rights reserved.

Scripture quotations marked TLB are taken from *The Living Bible* copyright © 1971. Used by permission of Tyndale House Publishers, Inc., Wheaton, Illinois 60189. All rights reserved.

The material presented in this book is not intended to replace professional counsel. Neither the publisher nor the author assumes responsibility for adverse consequences resulting from application of advice presented here.

Editor: Pam Pugh
Cover Design: John Hamilton
Interior Book Design: www.DesignByJulia
Interior Images: JupiterImages.com

Library of Congress Cataloging-in-Publication Data

Armstrong, Brenda.
   Financial relief for single parents : a proven plan for achieving
the seemingly impossible / by Brenda Armstrong.
       p. cm.
   Includes bibliographical references.
   ISBN-13: 978-0-8024-4409-7
   1. Finance, Personal--Religious aspects--Christianity. 2. Single
parents--Finance, Personal. I. Title.
HG179.A7244 2007
332.0240086'53--dc22

                                                                    2006032884

       ISBN: 0-8024-4409-1
       ISBN-13: 978-0-8024-4409-7

1 3 5 7 9 10 8 6 4 2

Printed in the United States of America

We hope you enjoy this book from Moody Publishers.
Our goal is to provide high-quality, thought-provoking books and products
that connect truth to your real needs and challenges.
For more information on other books and products written
and produced from a biblical perspective,
go to www.moodypublishers.com or write to:

Moody Publishers
820 N. LaSalle Boulevard
Chicago, IL 60610

TABLE OF CONTENTS

Foreword
A Word from the Author

The more life experience I gain and the more business knowledge I get, the more I am sure that the best people to learn from are those who have lived the thing they teach.

Business professors who have never actually run a business can have great theories on business. Those who write about parenting but have no everyday experience with kids can have great ideas. People who have never been married have plenty to say about marriage! But none of these people are the ones I want to learn from. I believe strongly in learning from experts who have been there, done that, and gotten the T-shirt. There is a wisdom that comes only from experience. The wisdom you get by actually doing is different than academics giving it their best guess.

When it comes to the dynamic of single parents and their money, Brenda Armstrong is the real deal. She has actually lived through the unique struggles, emotions, and victories of the single parent. If you are merely looking for highbrow concepts on money, this book isn't for you. This book is for people interested in the real thing.

Brenda is a writer who really understands from personal experience how scary money issues can be for the single parent. The single mothers and fathers I have met with and talked with on my radio show over the last two decades are people who often are fighting against rough times. They have emotions from the relationship that used to be, and those emotions affect how they approach money. Sometimes the problems are huge and fear is real, but these single parents press on. Much of the time money is short and fatigue is deep.

Single mothers and fathers need a voice spoken from true-life experience —someone who knows the problems are real, but so are the victories. They need someone who loves them enough to tackle tough subjects, but who is ministering to them along the way. *Financial Relief for Single Parents* is a real-world guide to a segment of our culture that needs the voice of experience to meet them where they are.

If you are a single parent or you love someone who is, then this is the book on finances to own and read. This material rooted in God's word is practical and it really works, every time. This is a book that will challenge you and inspire you, but not talk down to you, nor talk over your head.

Life transformation is almost always painful. The Bible says, "no discipline seems pleasant at the time, but it yields a harvest of righteousness." Brenda doesn't promise you an easy path to financial freedom, but if you want a process that works, brought to you by someone who knows from actually walking it, well . . . this book delivers.

Dave Ramsey
New York Times Bestselling Author of *The Total Money Makeover*

A Word From the Author

As you know, raising a family on two incomes is hard enough, let alone one. But you can do it. Congratulate yourself on picking up this book!

Your willingness to pick up this book shows your eagerness to assess and enhance your situation. As you journey through the process of doing so, you will discover a greater revelation of God's concern for you, your family, and your finances, and you will begin to have new hope.

Is God interested in your finances? Why would we think He cares about such things? Since Jesus said more about money and possessions than almost any other subject, we can consider that He must know that this is an important area of our lives. You might be surprised to learn that there are about 500 verses in the Bible about prayer, less than 500 about faith, and more than 2,350 verses on how to handle money and material possessions![1]

This book is designed to give you not only the tools you need to manage the resources you have, but the hope that you need to believe you can do it with God's help.

As you read through *Financial Relief for Single Parents*, you'll take a look at your financial goals and dreams, start to set up a spending plan, gain money-stretching ideas, learn biblical principles on money management, and take a look at your own unique, God-given personality and patterns as you consider your current job or next career move.

I owe a debt of gratitude to the late Larry Burkett, author of *Financial Guide for the Single Parent*. He was a champion for single parents and offered his expertise in the area of finances to help people in this situation. I learned much from him and many other wonderful Christian authors. My own insight into the unique needs of single parents comes from being one myself, as well as from working with single parents and training churches to help them.

Let's get started.

Brenda Armstrong

PART 1:
Foresight

CHAPTER 1

Let's Get Started

Setting Financial Goals

Maureen was watching television one evening and came across a program that featured a wealthy motivational speaker who was telling his audience how they, too, could find riches and happiness.

"If you don't set financial goals," he declared, "you won't reach any. Remember: If you aim at nothing, you're sure to hit it."

Financial goals? Maureen thought. *My goal is to get to payday with enough shampoo in the bottle that I don't have to water it down. Again. What planet is this guy on?*

Setting and achieving financial goals might seem like wishful thinking, but it is the first step in gaining control over your finances instead of having them control you. By putting your current situation in writing and establishing some goals — even small ones — you will gain a better perspective of your needs and new hope for being able to manage your finances. God will honor your efforts to manage your money His way.

What motivated you to pick up this book? Was it to provide for your children's needs? Was it to get out of debt? Or maybe your goal is to find practical ways to better manage your money and stretch your resources.

By writing out your goals, you may find you have one primary goal in mind and several secondary aims. So find a piece of paper or invest in a spiral notebook (on sale, of course!).

SETTING YOUR FINANCIAL GOALS

The main financial goal for anyone should be to live within his or her means. This may seem impossible now, but it simply means to spend no more than you make. This kind of financial freedom is possible—it really is.

Think of what this mother meant when she said, "Being a single parent is a mixed metaphor. It's riding the seesaw all by yourself, taking some real hard bumps and running around a lot to hold down someone else's end as well as your own. But it's also sliding down the slippery slide by yourself, going as fast or as slow or as often as you want."[2]

She said the slide part is that she doesn't have to see household money frittered away foolishly by someone else. Because she is the decision maker, she can set her own goals. And so can you.

Pray about your goals—not just in a quick, "Here's what I want from You" way, but as you spend time with God and grow in your relationship with Him, learn to hear His voice and follow His lead.

Maybe you're just beginning your walk with God, and it's a new concept to consider that God is interested in you and your family and your daily lives, let alone something like money.

Maybe you've been a Christian for a long time. Perhaps your circumstances have changed and you're looking to God to meet your needs in a new way.

Or it could be that you're just checking out spiritual things and haven't yet decided to follow Christ. Wherever you are, you can be assured that He knows you well and loves you. He is on your side. As one parent discovered, He is "Friend to the friendless. The number one pick for your team is Jesus. Reliance on Him is a slam-dunk; He won't refuse your request. Besides, He's on your team already."[3]

As you begin to consider financial goals, ask yourself these questions and others that you can think of so you know how finances fit into your values:

- What place does education hold in my future or in my children's future?

- How important is home ownership?

- What are my career goals? What further training do I need to reach these goals?

- How much time, money, and effort do I want to give to volunteer activities?

- What character traits do I value and want to develop in my life and the lives of my children?

- Are my financial goals in line with these traits?

- What are my retirement goals?

- How soon do I want to pay off debt?[4]

Some of your more immediate needs and challenges might include:

- Making housing expenses more manageable

- Improving credit

- Buying or repairing a car

- Buying or repairing appliances

- Getting a job that is more satisfying and/or pays more

- Finding better day/after-school care for the children

- Providing lessons, sports, or another activity for my child

- Pursuing hobbies

- Taking the family on vacation

- Others:

_____

_____

_____

_____

You may think it is unrealistic to make goals when you don't have enough for basic expenses, but I myself have been in impossible financial situations and can confirm that goal setting works.

When my kids were young I worked full time, but my income was stretched to afford a rental so bad that it required daily tacking up of tiles that were falling in the bathroom! In the kitchen the peeling wallpaper from the

"I'm so poor
I can't even pay attention."[5]

fifties revealed layers of unprofessionally installed designs. One thing I knew when I moved in was where to hang my pictures, because the holes were already in place.

My old clunker of a car finally died, and I had to rely on the kindness of co-workers and friends until it could be replaced. When the cupboards were nearly bare and the kids were wearing a size too small in clothing, I knew something needed to change. My goal, although I didn't know how I was going to reach it, was to be able to take care of my family's basic needs. Later, as my situation improved, other goals were added, and we eventually took our first real family vacation that didn't consist of pallets on the floor in the home of family members!

Considering what's important to you and writing your goals down is a good first step. You won't even know how to pray for your finances until you face them. To work toward any financial goal you must learn to live within your means. To do that, you must first get *wants*, *needs*, and *dreams* in their proper relationship.

God has promised to provide your needs, and often takes your wants and dreams into consideration. But let's start with the needs.

Needs are the purchases necessary to provide your basic requirements, such as food, clothing, shelter, and health.

Read Matthew 6:25–34, which begins with Jesus Himself saying, "Do not worry about your life, what you will eat or drink; or about your body, what you will wear" and assures you that "your heavenly Father knows that you need them." Look up this passage and read it through a few times. You might want to read it each morning and again at the end of the day. Get to know better this heavenly Father and the amazing certainty that He cares about your financial situation.

This truth is very comforting. God will provide for your needs. I often felt like my world was coming to an end. I remember crying out to God about what I did not have, and He would remind me that I had what I needed today—I had a roof over my head, I was clothed, and I had food to eat. I began to thank Him for those things, and I learned to trust Him to provide for my needs. "But if we have food and clothing, we will be content with that" (1 Timothy 6:8).

Taking time to be thankful for the basics is pleasing to Him and reminds us that He *has* provided. Keeping the Lord's faithfulness before us gives us courage to know He won't forget us tomorrow—or even later today! He often surprised my children and me with many of our wants and dreams, even many we had never spoken to Him about!

During a Bible study, a woman named Annette once said that being thankful and keeping perspective helped her. "When I start feeling sorry for myself and worrying, I remember that a lot of people are worse off than I am," she remarked. "Yes," replied her wise friend Marge, "but that doesn't change your own situation." Marge assured her that God cares for her situation too. Do not think your own situation has to be the worst in the world before God takes notice.

List some of your family's needs. You might even enlist your children to work on this with you.

_____

_____

_____

_____

_____

_____

You've probably listed the very basics. What else do you *need*? What do you need to get to work every day? A hair dryer? A car? Good walking shoes? Bus money?

Wants involve choices that extend beyond basic needs and include the quality of goods to be used. It's not wrong to have wants as long as we keep them all in perspective. You *need* a floor in your house, and you might *want* better carpeting. If your children are doing this exercise, remind them that they *need* protein but might *want* ice cream!

List some of your wants. These might also be some of your short-term goals.

_____

_____

_____

_____

_____

_____

 If your children are making their own lists, help them see how needs and wants often go together. For example, you might *need* a hair dryer to help you get ready for work or school in the morning—and you might *want* one that's red rather than white, but a different color is not a need!

Dreams are choices according to God's plan that can be made only out of surplus funds after all other obligations have been met. When you learn to give your wants and dreams to God, He changes your perspective. When you begin desiring what He wants for you, He often supplies much more than you need.

Psalm 37:4 tells us, "Delight yourself in the LORD and he will give you the desires of your heart." Let's not assume this assurance is a ticket for anything material we might like. After all, we're also admonished to "not love the world or anything in the world. If anyone loves the world, the love of the Father is not in him" (1 John 2:15).

The "world" is the world's system that puts myself first, that says this life is all there is, and that does not mind lying or hurting others as long as I and mine get what we're entitled to.

What might the psalmist be telling us, then, and how might these words relate to our finances? As we become closer to the Lord, and as we

Can you find an extra $2 or $3 a day? What if you made your own coffee instead of buying a cup? How about breakfast bars you get in the store instead of a doughnut at the bakery? Certainly you may treat yourself sometimes, but if you can hang on to a few dollars a day with the intention of putting it aside, you'll have something for a rainy day before you know it!

become more like Him, our desires will be more and more in line with His. Your dreams can be things that right now seem impossible, such as sending your children to college or going to college yourself. Perhaps you dream of owning your own home completely so that you have the financial freedom to do something productive in your retirement years without financial worries.

When you consider money not as something God has rewarded you with, but as something He's entrusted you with, you might dream of how you can give out of your surplus. Perhaps you and your children can dream of the day you can begin to sponsor a child through World Vision or another organization for thirty or forty dollars a month. These are the dreams and desires of the heart that please God.

OBSTACLES TO REACHING YOUR GOALS

Now that you have begun to consider some of your financial goals and, perhaps for the first time, have seen that God is interested in this area of your life, we need to briefly address some of the obstacles that may trip you up in your pursuit of your goals and dreams.

One obstacle is the fear of failure. Some people are so afraid of failing that they fall short of trying. And if you have failed in the past, don't let this stop you from trying again. After all, "the only way to avoid failure at all costs is to do nothing."[6] That's not what you want, is it?

You Can

BANK On It

It is God who is the source of all the needs of your life. Read the verses below. Read them again. Begin to memorize them.

"Do not worry, saying, 'What shall we eat?' or 'What shall we drink?' or 'What shall we wear?' For the pagans run after all these things, and your heavenly Father knows that you need them. But seek first his kingdom and his righteousness, and all these things will be given to you as well" (Matthew 6:31–33).

Another hindrance is low self-esteem. There are some people who feel that they are entitled to much—"After all, I deserve the best"—and that's not admirable, but on the other hand, there are people who struggle with the idea that they deserve any success. Do you remember the story of the Israelites whom God sent out to spy on the land He had promised them? The story is in Numbers 13. Most of the spies saw the people in the land as giants and themselves as grasshoppers and became afraid. God didn't see them as grasshoppers, but that's how they saw themselves. If low self-esteem is an obstacle for you, begin to work on developing a healthy self-evaluation.[7]

Some people think it's too late to begin setting goals, or that their goals will take too long or that they are too old. Remember that you can always improve and set new goals, no matter how old you are! Colonel Sanders and Mary Kay Ashe (founder of Mary Kay Cosmetics) were both well over fifty when they began their careers.[8]

And finally, sometimes we're just unwilling to change. We'd rather stay where we are than make a change. However, that's not you! You've already taken positive steps by picking up this book and reading it this far . . . and writing down or at least giving thought to the goals that are important to you.

PROFITABLE STEPS

■ Have a positive attitude about being able to set your own financial goals.

■ Look again at the lists on the previous pages and give serious thought to those things that are most important to you, both immediate and long term. Don't be afraid to dream!

■ Recognize God's ownership: God's Word tells us that God is the Provider and we are the steward of His resources. He gives us the talents and favor to earn money, but it all belongs to Him.

■ *"Yours, O LORD, is the greatness and the power and the glory and the majesty and the splendor, for everything in heaven is yours. Yours, O LORD, is the kingdom; you are exalted as head over all." (1 Chronicles 29:11)*

CHAPTER 2

Put It on Paper

Creating a Spending Plan

Chris says, "When my daughter was in 8th grade, she asked me how much money I made. Now, back in the day when I was young and asked that question of my father, I was told in no uncertain terms that it was none of my business. Period. Amen.

"But I decided to handle this question differently. I showed her a pay stub. She did not think it seemed like a lot of money, so she asked me how much it cost to live in our apartment. Never one to miss one of life's little learning opportunities, I handed her a pen and paper and said, 'Let's figure this out together.'

"So she put down how much my rent was, then electric, etc., until we had a negative balance. She said, 'Mom, you ran out of money before you paid everything. How do you do it?' I told her I borrowed from Peter to pay Paul. One month we pay all the utilities and no medical bills, the next month the medical bills and no utility bills. I explained that this was a very stressful way of living, and I hoped that she would not have to live this way when she grew up."

TELLING YOUR MONEY PART 1: SEE WHAT YOU SPEND

Chris's situation would have improved had she learned to create and stick to a budget and begun to understand

God's math. What is a budget? As John Maxwell says, "A budget is telling your money where to go, instead of wondering where it went."

A budget is a plan—a spending plan.

We know how much money we make, and we certainly know we spend it, and we think we have an idea where it goes, but without a written plan, we don't know for sure where it went.

Some people fear a written plan because they already know they do not have enough money to meet their expenses, and would rather not face the truth. But what you don't know *will* hurt you in the end. Think of writing your budget as being similar to starting on a trip — you cannot set a course without first determining where your starting point is.

Keep reading! Don't give up before you start. Don't think of this as an exercise of futility—think of it as an adventure in futurity! Think of working on your budget as an investment. Yes, it will take some time, but it's time well taken, and you're going to have a feeling of great satisfaction just for going through this experience. If you think you don't have time to make a budget, consider what financial counselor and author Dave Ramsey says to that: "You don't have time *not* to make a budget."

-----------------■-----------------

Dianne says, "One thing I have learned is how to budget my money. I worried a lot when my income dropped after my separation. But I learned to look at budgeting like dieting—I had to be creative and keep it under control because not doing it was disaster! People are constantly saying, 'I don't know how you do it!' I know it is a lesson that I will always be grateful for."

If you make plans and carry out your plans, a budget can do several things: make you more peaceful about your finances; help you determine what's most important to spend your money on; give you a taste of financial success; improve your self-confidence; make you a smarter consumer.[9]

And remember that your budget will become your financial lifestyle.

Facing the Figures

Let's take the first step, which is helping you see in black and white where your money is going now. You can use the form at the back of the book, make your own, write on a piece of paper, or get a form from the Internet.[10] You'll begin with your income from your job, but if you have other forms of regular income, such as bank interest, dividends, or child support you can consistently rely on to be paid, you can add those too. This will help you get a big picture of all available funds you have to use.

We'll work with your gross income; that is, your income before taxes and any other payroll deductions are taken out. If the amount you are paid is consistent from month to month, you can figure out your gross pay by multiplying your last gross amount times twenty-four or twelve or by however many paychecks you get each year.

If you do not receive a pay stub or your pay will not have changed significantly from last year, you can also find out your gross pay by looking at last year's income tax return.

Write down all of your income.

Keeping Track

Keeping good records will allow you to see where you are; make necessary changes in your financial habits; and, having set goals, find encouragement in the progress you're making.

Keep reading. You might want to read all the way through this chapter before you write anything down to get an idea of what you'll be working on. The important thing is to *keep going!*

Now you're ready to determine how much you're spending. We're not quite ready to "tell the money where to go," but we're going to take a look at where it does go. Anything you pay out of your income is an expense, and each expense will be deducted from your gross income.

Giving

One of the most important areas of expenses is charitable giving. We'll talk more about giving later, but for now, write down the amount you currently give.

Taxes

As the old saying goes, death and taxes are two things we can be certain of. Unless the government decides to do away with payroll taxes, this is an obligation everyone with an income has whether it is taken out of your pay or not. There have been many changes in the tax laws in recent years, so it's difficult to put a percentage on the taxes a working single parent pays.

Look at last year's tax return and find out how much was withheld. If you overpaid and received a refund, subtract one from the other and you'll know what you are actually paying.

God tells us to pay our taxes and to give, as we'll explain later. These are non-negotiables for those who follow Him. With that in mind, the money you have left after you figure these is typically your Net Spendable Income—the part God has given you to manage. However, to keep things simple, we're going to include these with all other expenses.

Savings

Count all that you are currently saving, either through a payroll deduction or directly to the bank or credit union. Don't forget Christmas club savings! If you are not currently saving—don't be discouraged. You'll find ways to begin as you continue your adventure.

Fixed Expenses

When reviewing what your monthly expenses are, you'll see that some are fixed and others are variable. Fixed expenses are not hard to figure because these are those that do not change from month to month, so jot them down. Remember that you might not have any expenses in certain categories and you might have expenses that are not listed.

Some of your fixed expenses are:

- housing (mortgage or rent; homeowner's or renter's insurance; real estate taxes)
- car payment, auto insurance, license, taxes

- regular insurance premiums (medical, dental, life)
- tuition
- childcare
- other

If you are on a budget plan with a utility company and you pay the same amount each month, consider these fixed expenses. Otherwise, look over your checkbook for the past several months and figure what you have been paying for electricity, heat, water, trash pickup, telephone, cable, and anything else. If you can't find records of these payments, the utility companies can provide the amounts you have paid over the year.

When determining your total housing expenses, include these:

- electricity
- gas
- water
- trash pickup
- telephone
- cell phone
- cable TV
- other

Once you've accumulated records of a year's worth of payments, add them up and divide that number by twelve. Now you know how much you're paying on average per month in these categories.

Variable Expenses

Some expenses are those unruly ones that aren't paid every month. These are variable expenses and not quite as easy to figure out.

Certain car costs are a good example of variable expenses. Figure out what you typically pay for gasoline in your car as well as oil, tires, licenses, taxes, if applicable, and maintenance. Add these costs when determining your total auto expenses:

- gasoline
- oil
- tires
- maintenance
- licenses, tags, and taxes (if applicable)

If you have credit card debt, record what you have been paying per month. Record any other loans or debts that have not been mentioned.

- credit cards
- other loans (student, personal, bank)

Many people underestimate the expenses of

- food/groceries (also include cleaning supplies and nonedible necessities such as soap, shampoo, toilet paper)
- clothing (include shoes, underwear, etc.)

You may sometimes feel you don't have any entertainment! But figure you spend something to enjoy life a little. Expenses like these can be classified as miscellaneous when you record your expenses:

- morning coffee and doughnut
- eating out, concerts, events
- movies, DVD rentals
- field trips
- vacation, camping
- sports, lessons, hobbies, activities, club dues and fees, costumes, uniforms, equipment
- other

Other expenses that cannot be forgotten can include, but not be limited to:

- school supplies
- medical—co-pay for doctor's visits, deductibles, tests, eye exams and glasses
- prescriptions, and so on; in other words, medical expenses that are not covered by your insurance
- haircuts
- dry cleaning/Laundromat
- gifts
- allowances
- subscriptions
- other

Counting the Cost

It is nearly impossible to know what you spend without first tracking it. Lynn insisted that she was very conservative with her budget and that she didn't spend any on luxuries. She was frugal, but because she bought her daily fix of gum with her groceries, it slipped her mind. She spent over $100 a year on the stuff! Money slips through our fingers in many ways when we do not have a payment to record. A checkbook is not the only way to keep track of spending, because we combine so many expenses. In other words, we may record a withdrawal of $30, but we have no record of how that $30 was spent. Was it for gasoline or snacks? something for the kids? Anyway, you may be one of the many people who are notorious for not keeping track of debit receipts and consequently, not recording them.

The only way to properly track everything you spend is to keep a journal for a minimum of one month and preferably for three, listing every amount that was spent, down to the penny. Buy a small spiral notebook or whatever works for you, write the date on the first page, and record: notebook $.85.

This habit will give you a surprising look at where money is going and where it sometimes melts away.

PROFITABLE STEP

■ If you are not able to pay your bills because of lack of money or from overspending, you are in financial bondage. This is what the Bible means by saying that a borrower is a slave to the lender. However, true financial freedom comes from learning to become a good steward. A steward cares for something that belongs to someone else. By diligently and prayerfully working through your spending plan, you are taking a hugely profitable step!

YOU CAN
BANK ON IT

Since everything you have really belongs to God, being a good steward means managing well the money God has entrusted to you. God has decided what you will have, and He has a way for you to manage it. It is possible, even if your income is low, but it's only possible if you look at your situation realistically and plan ahead. A good spending plan, or budget, requires action and consistency to make it work. It may require sacrifice initially. Remember the old adage: if we fail to plan, we are planning to fail. So begin the planning now! Be patient and remember that budgeting is a process, and it can take up to nine months to a year to finalize a workable spending plan. Your goal is to live within your means.

Telling Your Money Part 2: Spending Plan Guidelines

Now that you have an idea of where your money goes, let's figure out what percentages of your income you should be spending for each expense.

The percentages in the guideline budget suggest how much of an average single parent's income ideally would be set aside for each expense in a comfortable budget. There are a lot of differences in family situations, income levels, and needs, so your percentages may vary from those in the guideline budget. Also, your budget will vary depending on your area of the country (for example, whether state taxes are collected or the cost of housing is higher or lower). Remember that not all of these expenses will be filled in; for example, you might not have investments, or you might not have childcare costs.

> "What can be measured can be understood. What can be understood can be altered."
>
> Katherine Neville

The following are suggested guidelines a single parent should follow. Remember that wherever the expenses of your spending plan fall within these ranges, your total percentages must not exceed 100 percent. Be sure to take into consideration the notes under childcare and investments.

- Housing — 25 to 35 percent
- Groceries/household supplies — 10 to 15 percent
- Auto — 12 to 15 percent
- Insurance — 3 percent
- Debts — 5 percent
- Entertainment — 5 to 7 percent
- Clothing — 5 to 6 percent
- Savings — 5 percent
- Medical/dental — 4 to 5 percent

- Miscellaneous — 5 to 8 percent
- School/childcare* — 0 to 15 percent
- Investments** — 0 to 13 percent

* Childcare costs can vary tremendously. If your workday more or less over-laps your child's school day, any costs you might have in this area will not be as high as they are when you must pay for all-day care. As a single parent, you'll want to provide the best childcare you can for your children, given your accessible resources. You might have family members who take care of your children while you work, or older siblings who care for the younger ones. You'll work out this aspect of your spending plan according to your own situation. For our purposes here, we have factored in a childcare cost of 0 percent. If you do have this expense, you'll have to jiggle the numbers to work out your percentages to not exceed 100.

** You may not be ready to invest any funds, or you may qualify for an auto-matic deduction for investments through your employer.

Sharpen your pencil, put on your "math hat," and see how your payments measure up against these guidelines. Don't forget that this is a model, not an absolute law of the universe.

If, for example, your gross income is $3,000 a month and you're spending $1,020 on all your housing expenses, divide 1020 by 3000. You get .34, or 34 percent of your income on housing.

Complete the same exercise with your other bills and expenses.

> ## PROFITABLE STEP #1

■ If you are someone who glazes over at the thought of writing down numbers, calculating percentages, and so on, you are not alone! Believe it or not, there are plenty of people who enjoy working with numbers. Try contacting your church to find someone who can help you work out your percentage guidelines.

> PROFITABLE STEP #2

■ At this point, you might be weary of numbers running through your head. Don't be disheartened. You are simply beginning to see why your situation has caused you stress. Keep reading — there are answers for you. You'll learn how to make the most of the resources you have. You'll begin to feel more confident and ready to work out a feasible spending plan.

The guideline budget helps you compare what you *are* spending with what you *should be* spending. You'll be able to see where you are overspending and where you can make cuts and adjustments. If you are overspending, the percentage guideline can be used as a goal for budgeting and also shows where you will want to set a limit in a particular category. Once you've determined where your money is going — and where too much of it is going — you can decide what areas can be reduced to limit overspending or adjusted to work within an income that is too small to stretch over your current spending patterns.

Making It Fit

Look at what you are spending now compared to what you should be spending. If you feel stretched to the limit and discouraged, this is a good time to consider finding a mentor, a friend who is good at finances, or a trained budget coach to help you analyze your budget and make wise decisions. There are organizations you can contact to request assistance from a qualified budget coach near you.[11]

After comparing what you're now spending with what you should be spending, you are ready to take the next step: develop a budget, or spending plan, that reflects changes that need to be made. A new budget will help you to control spending in certain areas, or at least reduce it, so you can live within your means. In the next chapters, you'll find ideas on stretching your income to fit your new budget.

It is not necessary that your new budget fit the guideline budget. *What is important is that your new budget does not exceed 100 percent of your gross income!* Basic expenses of housing, auto, and food must not add to up more than 60 percent of your spending plan or you will find it very difficult, if not impossible, to manage your other expenses. Your goal in creating a workable spending plan is to provide for your family by living within your means and without using debt.

Remember Chris, who told her grade school daughter that she made ends meet by borrowing from Peter to pay Paul? Her daughter learned a better way: "Elizabeth isn't following in my footsteps. Instead, she is using the life lessons we had, and she will not put anything on her credit card until the last purchase is paid in full. If she can't afford to go out to dinner or a movie, she invites a friend over for games and popcorn.

"I think in our situation it was important to share how much my salary was with her and how much it was costing to live. I wasn't getting child support regularly and had a lot of medical bills because she was sick the first four years of her life. So my motto has always been: Don't blow your kids off when they come seeking knowledge or asking questions, as this may discourage them from asking or seeking."

It is very important to teach children while they are young. They can learn about money on their own level, but you won't want them to carry your adult burdens.

Now let's get into more specifics about various expenses of your spending plan and how to make the most of what you have.

You Can
BANK On It

Plans fail for lack of counsel, but with many advisers they succeed (Proverbs 15:22). Commit to the LORD whatever you do, and your plans will succeed (Proverbs 16:3).

wisdom

CHAPTER 3

Necessities

Giving, Taxes, Saving

There is a story of a man who had one brown cow and one white cow. He was going to give one of them to God, but hadn't yet decided which one. Then one of the cows was attacked by wolves and killed. The man sorrowfully went to God in prayer: "I'm sorry, Lord. It's a shame that Your cow died."[12]

THE TITHE

You and I probably don't struggle with which cow to give to the Lord. However, we might struggle with the concept of giving at all, especially when our resources are already stretched, when we're in debt, and when our bills are overwhelming. But giving back to God a portion of what He has provided is something He asks of every Christian.

Our attitude when giving is important, perhaps as important as the amount we give. In Jesus' day, the Pharisees would figure out their tithe all the way to the mint leaves in their gardens. But when the Lord looked into their hearts, He saw that they had "neglected the more important matters of the law—justice, mercy and faithfulness." Yes, giving their tithe was important, but they "should have practiced the latter, without neglecting the former" (Matthew 23:23).

The point is that God expects us to give, but expects our gifts to come from a heart of love for Him.

Second Corinthians 9:7 says that "Each one of you should give what you have decided in your heart to give, not reluctantly or under compulsion, for God loves a cheerful giver" (TNIV).

Why does God expect us to give? He certainly doesn't need our money. He asks for a portion of it for our spiritual health and to provide resources for His work. Your giving is an outward sign that shows how much you trust God and His provision in your heart. The first step in trusting Him is recognizing that He owns it all; He has decided how much you will have to manage, and He has a plan to help you do so.

It's not easy to get in the habit of writing a check for a tithe or offering before other obligations when your money is tight. However, giving is a principle that God has instituted for our good, and lack of giving shows that something is lacking in our relationship with God.

The tithe—10 percent—is a guideline that comes from the Old Testament when the Israelites were required to set aside this portion of their produce. You can read about this in Deuteronomy 26. The point is that they were to give the firstfruits of what they had—not the leftovers.

The idea behind writing your check to God's work first is to give to Him above all other things. And He promises to meet your needs if you do so. An intriguing passage in Malachi is the only time God asks us to test Him: "'Bring the whole tithe into the storehouse, that there may be food in my house. Test me in this,' says the LORD Almighty, 'and see if I will not throw open the floodgates of heaven and pour out so much blessing that you will not have room enough for it'" (3:10).

Someone asked financial counselor Dave Ramsey if she should tithe when there were debts and other bills to pay. He replied, "Honestly, if you can't live on 90 percent, it's unlikely that you can live on 100 percent. . . . Pray and read the Bible and let God speak to you on this. But this point is clear: The Bible doesn't say wait until you get your debt under control, it says tithe—first fruits off the top before anything else."[13]

Pray about your giving. If you're stuck on the 10 percent and that is preventing you from giving because you don't believe you'll make it on the remainder, begin by giving something from each paycheck or each time you receive money from any source. Giving is a matter of the heart, and God may be calling you to a greater level of faith. One writer says, "You can't afford not to give — especially those of you who are in debt. I can't explain it except to say that when you honor God with your giving, something supernatural happens. Living off 90 percent of your income allows God to step in and make it go further than 100 percent."[14]

Patrice, a single mother of three children, states, "My tithe is a considerable amount of money when there is so little to spare. But I have found when I tithe, somehow the bills get paid even when it seems impossible. But if I don't tithe, then the worries come. I find careless spending is more of a temptation. Then I get behind on the bills. But when I've stuck to the tithe, my children and I have always had plenty to eat and good clothes to wear."

You Can **Bank** On It

"Whoever sows sparingly will also reap sparingly, and whoever sows generously will also reap generously" (2 Corinthians 9:6). *Having a goal of tithing your income is a worthy one, and you'll be blessed when you achieve it.*

I do not know your personal situation, your background, or your beliefs. I know that Christians have different points of view on the matter of tithing and giving offerings. Some people will teach that you must give 10 percent of your gross paycheck; others will say that we should give 10 percent of net, and still others will say that the 10 percent is only a guideline and that as Christians in the age of grace we're not under compulsion to give any set amount. I cannot tell you what to do. I can only share with you what Scripture says and what others have discovered when they have made tithing a goal.

The 10 percent guide is just that—a guide. It's the intent that matters in the Lord's sight. You might one day be in a position to joyfully give more.

Taxes

The Bible is clear that we are to "give to Caesar [the government] what is Caesar's" (Mark 12:17). We have to pay our taxes. Of course we want to make sure we only pay what we legitimately owe.

Chances are that your income and your taxes are straightforward. But whatever your situation, do not give in to the temptation to be less than honest. "If you owe taxes, pay taxes," advises our practical Bible in Romans 13:7.

It is beyond the scope of this book to discuss taxes at length. For routine situations, you can find affordable at-home tax software programs that are reliable and user-friendly. If you have a home-based business or are otherwise self-employed; or if your situation is complicated; or if you just need advice on exemptions, deductions, and filling out your tax return, you should seek the help of a professional. Tax laws change often, and help is available.[15] It's a good idea to become familiar with some basics of taxes.

Filing: If you qualify as head of household, file as head of household rather than as a single taxpayer. Head of household status carries lower tax rates, allowing you to take advantage of a larger standard deduction.[16]

Exemptions: Exemptions are the amount you can subtract from your income and reduce your taxable income. For example, you can be an exemption, as can your dependents.

Deductions: Expenses that the government lets you subtract from your income, either as a standard deduction or as an itemized deduction.

The standard deduction is determined by your income and marital status when filing your taxes. The standard deduction is listed in the instruction book that is mailed with your tax forms and is automatically figured for you in the tax software programs, or you can check to find the current year's deduction.

If you own a home, you might have enough deductions to itemize them—you can list (and must document or provide proof of) your mortgage interest, property taxes, charitable donations, some medical expenses, some work-related expenses, and so on. Generally speaking, if your itemized deductions add up to a sum higher than your standard deduction, you should itemize. Otherwise, use the standard deduction.

Tax Credit: Tax credits are different from deductions. Deductions adjust, or reduce, the amount of income you must pay taxes on. Once the tax obligation from the adjusted taxable income has been determined, tax credits can reduce the amount of tax you owe. For example, you can deduct a certain amount from your taxable income for each dependent under seventeen. You may qualify for a credit for childcare expenses or certain retirement plan contributions. Check www.irs.gov for the current year's credits. You may also qualify for a credit on contributions you have made to a retirement savings account.[17]

If you have a college student in the family, you might qualify for the Hope Scholarship and/or the Lifetime Learning Credit. Once again, you should seek the best and most current information.[18]

Earned Income Credit: One tax break you should be aware of and for which many single-parent families qualify is the Earned Income Credit (EIC) or Earned Income Tax Credit. This credit is for people who earn low to moderate incomes. As the IRS says on its Web site, "Working families and individuals may keep more of what they work for." EIC is a tax incentive for lower-income working families that reduces federal taxes to as low as 0 percent, and some families receive refunds above what was paid in federal taxes. If you qualify, you can take a lump sum credit as a refund when you file your taxes, or you can spread it out over the year by applying for Advanced Income Credit.

Withholding: Most employers withhold an amount from your pay for federal, state, and local taxes. Ideally, you will pay exactly the amount of tax you owe. In other words, you won't underpay through your payroll withholdings and owe money to the IRS, and you won't overpay and find that the government owes you a refund.

"Intaxication—
Euphoria at getting a refund
from the IRS, which lasts
until you realize it was your
money to start with."[19]

Some people like getting a refund, but all that means is that the government took too much in the first place and they are returning what they borrowed from you interest free. It would have been better if you had had that amount throughout the year to work with or to add to your savings account.

If your employer does not withhold taxes for you or you are self-employed, it is still your responsibility to make sure you hold back enough to pay taxes when they are due. The government may require that you pay on a quarterly basis, but if not you can still do so. Just make sure that you are paying only what is necessary.

SAVING

After you have taken care of your giving to the Lord and giving to Caesar, you should put something back for a rainy day or for one of those goals you dreamed about when you began this adventure. You may start out slowly, and you'll find that by getting in the habit of setting something aside from each paycheck, it becomes easier over time.

If you have direct deposit as an option for receiving your paycheck, you can also have an amount deducted automatically and put into a savings account or credit union.

Why save? For one thing, it's a good discipline. Proverbs describes the hardworking ants who "labor hard all summer, gathering food for the winter" (6:8 NLT).

Saving makes provision for the future, for those days when you have an emergency, whether that is a repair bill, illness, or something drastic such as loss of a job. It is also the means of accomplishing some of those goals you had in mind.

Many advisers recommend having a goal of saving two or three months of your income in a readily accessible account. For a single parent, this will seem like an unrealistic number—and it may well be. However, the point is to begin now, no matter how small the amount.

Your first goal should be to accumulate $1,000 in savings for emergencies. You can do that in one year if you can cut just $20 a week from your budget; in two years if you can only manage $10 week.

Often when there is an emergency and there are no savings to draw from, people use their credit cards. Think of saving as *providing* for the future and debt as *borrowing* from the future.

Do your best not to treat your savings account like a backup checking account to run to when your checking account gets low.

Your bank might have a savings plan for children. You'll want to check into that and get your children into the habit of saving as they begin to earn or are given money of their own.

One father gave each child four banks. Whenever the child got money, whether it was from allowance, gifts, or from extra chores, the amount was to be divided four ways: 10 percent went into one bank to be given away; 30 percent was for spending; 30 percent was for short-term savings for items such as a new bicycle or DVD player; 30 percent was for long-term savings—this would be kept aside for purchases later in life such as a car, foreign travel, or college expenses.

One parent reported that her daughter used the money she had saved up in her long-term bank for a two-week missions trip to Mexico with her youth group.

> ## PROFITABLE STEP

■ How much is in your pocket or purse right now? Can you take a part of that amount and stash it away?

CHAPTER 4

Walls, Wheels, & What's to Eat?

Housing, Car, Groceries

You must live somewhere. And what, after all, makes a home? It's where you live, where your family has its stuff, where you run into those you love in the hallway, and where the table is. "A house that does not have one worn, comfy chair in it is soulless."[20]

HOUSING

Housing expenses are made up of everything you need to keep your home running and safe, which include rent or mortgage, home insurance, taxes, maintenance and repairs, and utilities. Your primary phone can go in this category too, but not cell phones for the kids! Ideally, the amount of your gross income that goes to housing should not exceed 35 percent. This percent will vary from family to family in different parts of the country, but it is a good guideline to follow. If you find yourself spending more than half your income on housing expenses over the long term, it will be extremely difficult to live within a balanced budget, especially for parents who have childcare expenses.

Single parents on stretched incomes have become very creative in keeping a roof over their heads. Consider the following to determine the best housing option for your family and ways to reduce your housing costs.

Buying a Home

Since the cost of suitable housing for your family is perhaps the greatest expense you'll ever incur, you must study your personal situation, research the possibilities, and pray for the Lord's guidance in order to make an educated decision about finding what's right for you.

There are many benefits to owning your own home. The most obvious one is that instead of making payments for someone else's property, as you are by renting, you are investing in your own. You will gain equity on the house, and your house will almost always appreciate in value. At tax time, you can write off all the interest you pay to the mortgage company and any points and fees paid to the lender at the time of closing. A home is probably the greatest investment you'll ever make.

If you think that buying a home may be the right decision for your situation, you should consult with a licensed real estate agent. Be sure your job is secure enough to take on a mortgage. And in considering a location, you'll want to buy with the idea of living in the space at least five years, especially if you're a first-time owner with a low down payment. Equity and resale value in this case would be a loss if sold in less time. The real estate agent can tell you about the economy of the area and resale opportunity, and you'll also want to know how much the property taxes are and if they could be raised substantially. Check on the cost of living if the area is unfamiliar to you.

As with every step you take, you need to prayerfully consider this decision and seek the counsel of other believers.

Your real estate agent can show properties that could otherwise be unavailable, but the services of the agent primarily come into play during the period of negotiation with the seller or listing agent. These negotiations take a certain level of expertise and help prevent mistakes commonly made by buyers who do not have such representation.

You have many options for the type of home you can buy, such as new house, existing house, handyman's special, condominium, mobile home, and prebuilt home.

New House

As with everything else, there are ups and downs of building your own house.

On the upside, you can design your house to fit your family's needs and choose your location. On the downside, you usually spend more money than you had planned, and it takes considerable time and mental effort to oversee the construction.

Building in a predesigned subdivision is a little easier because the plans are already set and the builder offers much fewer options to consider.

Existing House

When you buy an existing house—or "pre-owned," as the contract will say—you know the cost up front. A house that has been lived in already has curtains, curtain rods, towel racks, lights in the closets, an established lawn, and shrubbery. Appliances are sometimes included with the house, or sold to the buyer by the owner, but be sure the contract states exactly what will remain in the house when the sellers move out.

The fellow that owns his own home is always just coming out of a hardware store.[21]

There are also some disadvantages—a home that has been lived in will naturally have some wear and tear and might even need repairs. Your home inspector can tell you the condition of the structure and major areas of concern, such as the heating and air-conditioning, roof, hot water heater, and appliances.

Handyman's Special

In real estate lingo, a house might be described as a fixer-upper or a handyman's special. This house will be more economical than one that is in prime condition, but you need to consider the cost of repairs and remodeling. Before you make a commitment, be sure to find out exactly what needs to be done. If you have skills and enjoy this kind of challenge, a fixer-upper might be right for you. Just keep in mind that repairs usually cost more and take more time than you had originally planned. However, when you're finished, you'll have a nice home and should even make a profit when it's time to sell.

Condominiums and Town Houses

These can be a doable option for purchasing your own home. You need to be aware of any additional costs involved above the purchase price, such as annual association fees, club fees, and any other amenities available in the community. Be aware that fees are subject to change year to year, and you have no control over them. A home like this is not a bad option, especially if you don't want to bother with yard work or shoveling snow. Another advantage is that you'll be a homeowner, and many times condominiums in towns or suburbs are more reasonably priced than houses. Traditionally these offered lower resale value than independent homes, but they are gaining value in some cities.

Mobile Homes or Prebuilt Homes

Although some people won't consider living in manufactured or "pre-fab" homes because of preconceived notions about this type of housing, many families have purchased them and think they are great. These options give people better housing than they could otherwise afford and satisfy the needs of their families. Trailers of yesteryear were unsafe tin cans. But today's models meet high safety standards and offer modern amenities.

The major disadvantage of manufactured housing is the depreciation. A new prebuilt home will lose about 25 percent of its total value when it leaves the sales lot. Consider purchasing a previously owned manufactured home rather than a newly built unit, because someone else has already taken the depreciation. Since you can decide to place your home on your own lot or in a subdivision or park, you'll want to look for areas that are not depressed, because you might not be able to easily find a buyer when it's time for you to sell and move on.

Purchase Options

Ultimately, your goal should be to become debt free—including your home. Most families cannot pay cash for the full amount for their first home and must borrow the money, but you should make it your goal to pay it off as soon as possible. As you look at financing your home, you will quickly discover the myriad of mortgage options available today. Because this can be a confusing area to navigate, most communities or lenders offer free classes to potential buyers to help them understand the best option for them.

Mortgage options can get kind of crazy! You can borrow your down payment (not recommended) with one loan; get another for your closing; another for your private mortgage insurance (PMI); and another for your mortgage. Imagine the pressure to make sure each is paid because they are all secured with the house; one missed payment could cause you to lose your home.

People who want to eventually have a debt-free home usually begin by purchasing a starter home. They buy the best small house they can get for the least amount of money, put a great deal of time and effort into it, improve its value, sell it, and then buy perhaps a larger and more expensive house after five years or so. This plan works well as long as the economy is good and home sales continue to rise, but you have to realize that this may be your longer-term home if the economy drops.

Your home is a shelter and not an investment strategy. However, homes generally do increase in value and can be a very good investment because there is a return. But your goal should not be to make money on your home; it should be to provide the best housing you can afford for your family.

Loans

Loans are based on a variety of factors, including your income, work stability, and credit score.

Loans are available through banks, savings and loans, credit unions, or mortgage companies. As mentioned, there are so many variables in mortgage opportunities that you need to research all the types of loans available to you and what additional costs are associated with each. Something to seriously consider is that most applications include a place for you to include the child support you receive as part of your income. The amount you are loaned is based on income, and if that income is not secure, you may default quickly and lose your home. Only about half the child support orders are paid in full. Something happens—a job change, illness, a move—and the support stops. So, don't include your child support as income unless you can afford the risk.

Your credit score depends upon your credit history. Have you ever borrowed money or had a credit card? Have you ever been late with a payment? If so, how often? You can pull your credit history from any of the three major credit reporting bureaus and obtain your credit score to see how you are rated.

Fees and Contracts

To keep a seller from selling a house you would like to buy, you will need to put down "earnest money." Under many contracts you will lose the money if the loan does not go through. However, you can word your contract to be contingent on the approved mortgage, which means you will get it back if the loan is not approved.

Most mortgages require a down payment—usually between 5 percent for first-time buyers to 20 percent, but if you can you should put more down. At the signing of the contracts at closing, there are additional costs, which include loan origination fees, points, attorneys' fees, survey fees, appraisal fees, PMI (private mortgage insurance), real estate commissions, credit reports, title search fees, and more. These fees can add up to several thousand dollars and should be researched thoroughly when considering any loan. Many times the seller may pay for some or all of the closing costs.

If your offer to purchase the home is subject to selling your present home, getting financial approval, or waiting on results from various inspections, including radon gas testing, termite inspections, appliance and structural inspections, or water testing, be sure each of these contingencies are spelled out in the contract.

Fixed rate loans are the "safest" types of mortgages, even though the rate is slightly higher. You know exactly what the interest rate and monthly mortgage payment will be and if they will fit into your budget. Most lenders allow extra payments on principal without penalty, which means your equity grows quicker than other loan types. The only variation will be the escrow account, where your creditor keeps the funds to pay your home insurance and taxes. These increase as the value of the home increases.

ARM (adjustable rate mortgage) loans may be a good option for you if you have a large down payment. The interest rate is initially lower, but it can fluctuate several percentage points higher than a fixed rate mortgage, depending on the economy. Therefore, it's very important to know exactly how high the interest rate could go. Plus, many of these loans are short-term loans that carry a balloon payment (typically due in seven years). This option is risky and only works for people who know they can pay off the home in that amount of time. There is no guarantee you'll be able to renegotiate another loan you can afford, and you could lose your home.

Payday mortgages are designed to increase the frequency of your loan payments. Instead of paying a monthly payment, the home buyer pays one-half the monthly payment every other week or one-quarter of the payment every week. Since more of the payment is applied to the principal, equity is accrued at a faster rate. This will consequently reduce the life of the loan, and the borrower reaps the benefits of paying less interest and paying off the mortgage early. Some lenders don't offer this type of loan, because they lose interest. However, there are independent companies that offer plans you can purchase to pay this way. Costs vary but are usually reasonable at around $300 for the life of the loan.

An interest-only mortgage is in general not advisable since you won't be paying down your principal. However, if you are looking to buy a house for a short-term situation in an area where rental costs are high, it may be an option to consider.

An assumable mortgage is an existing mortgage that is assumed, or taken on, by the buyer with the existing terms of the seller's loan. Assumable mortgages benefit the buyer because the interest rate and mortgage payment are usually lower than current rates. Some owners can afford to let the buyers lease with option to buy, which cuts down the loaned amount. However, other owners may require a higher down payment up front to cover their equity. Check to see if there is an assumption fee and if the loan will be assumable if you sell the home to someone else.

Government loans, such as VA and FHA, are available to some buyers. Other mortgage options that might benefit you are land contract, trust deed, or equity sharing.

> ### PROFITABLE STEP

■ If you are planning on becoming a homeowner, do as much research as you can so you'll make wise decisions.

SELLING YOUR HOME

If you are on the other side of the coin and determine that you must sell a home instead of purchasing one, you must first decide if you will sell your home yourself or hire a real estate agent. You can save the cost of an agent's commission if you sell it yourself, but you are responsible for the advertising and showing of the home to interested buyers. You need to know what other homes in your area are selling for and understand what you must do when someone contracts to buy it. Have a qualified attorney review all offers before you sign anything.

Using a realty company gives your home greater exposure in the real estate market.

Properties that are listed by a licensed real estate agent are presented to a much wider audience through the Multiple Listing Service (MLS), as well as marketed through multiple channels that are not available when selling by owner. One of the most important factors in using a real estate agent for buying or selling is having the paperwork done for you. You can drastically reduce your chance of legal action taken against you for a sale gone wrong with the use of a real estate agent who handles these types of documents on a daily basis.

In addition, properties sold by a licensed agent, sell on average, for 10 to 15 percent more than a house sold by the owner.

Financial Considerations When Selling Your Home

Continued liability: You can be held liable for any loan a buyer assumes from you if the buyer defaults, unless you obtain a total release from liability. Contact the lending institution for more information about obtaining one of these releases. Check to see if there is a fee involved.

Potential buyers are putting up earnest money for a home they are serious about buying, and you should be willing to explain any problems or situations the buyer should know about. Not only will it save the buyer some headaches down the road, but you will be setting a wonderful Christian example. This is the time to declare which items will be included, such as appliances, curtains, swing sets, firewood, or maintenance equipment.

OTHER "HOUSEKEEPING" ITEMS

Refinancing

If you are considering refinancing and want to see if it will actually save you money, figure the dollar amount of interest you will save compared to the costs involved in refinancing. Some banks will require closing costs for the new loan for new title searches, surveys, and appraisals. If you can easily reclaim these expenses through the savings in interest within a few years, refinancing is for you. You usually will benefit through refinancing if the new interest rate is at least 3 percent lower than your present mortgage.

Home Equity Loan

If you already have a mortgage, your mailbox is probably full of offers for second mortgages, and you may be wondering if you should take advantage of them, especially to pay off consumer debts. Although the idea is tempting, you'll incur more debt, and many homeowners have lost their property through inability to pay off another loan. Borrowing more money, especially against the equity in your home, doesn't usually solve the problem.

Foreclosure

If you have not been able to make your mortgage payments, make every effort to work out something with the lender. However, if foreclosure is inevitable, try your best to sell your home, even if you have to take a loss. Since foreclosed dwellings are generally sold at auction for much less than fair market value, you often can sell it for more, thus reducing the amount you must pay back.

Buying a Foreclosed Home

Buying a foreclosed home is a concern for some people because they think they are taking advantage of the person who is losing their home. In practical fact, these people are going to lose their homes regardless of whether you buy them out of foreclosure, because the bank is going to foreclose. As long as you did not generate the foreclosure, there is nothing scripturally wrong with buying a foreclosed dwelling. If you can get to the family before they get into foreclosure, you could save them some money they might lose otherwise.

Remember, however, that in many instances the family will already have moved out of the house and it has been vacant. Since a house can quickly fall into disrepair—and an unoccupied house is a target for vandalism—you might have to consider the cost of repairs into the amount you're paying for the house.

Home Insurance

Most lending institutions require that you have enough insurance to cover the amount of the mortgage, minimum liability, and damage to the property. However, a comprehensive homeowner's policy is recommended because it covers the home, more extensive liability and damage to property and contents, and is usually the least expensive way to insure a dwelling. Shop around before you buy any kind of insurance, because there can be a significant amount of difference in the cost of insurance from one company to another. This insurance is usually included in your escrow payment along with your principal and interest payments to the lender each month, who then pays the payments when due.

Prepaying Your Mortgage

After you have made your regular monthly payment, any additional funds you put toward your mortgage go directly to the principal, exclusive of any interest. There are some mortgage calculators used by lenders that can help you determine the sizable savings. You can find these on lenders' Web sites. Before making any prepayments on your mortgage, check with your lending institution about any penalties, and request an annual amortization schedule to monitor the reduction in your principal balance.

RENTING A HOME

If you have decided that renting is currently a better option for you, you need to consider several things, such as what type of residence, location, being willing to share a residence with another person or family, and cost of rentals in the area. The people in your church are often a good source of information for some of these.

Types of Leases

There are two basic types of leases: month-to-month lease or one for a specified amount of time—usually six months or one year. The month-to-month lease is great if you aren't sure how long you will need the space, but realize that the rent can be raised with only a 30-day notice. You can avoid this problem with a six-month or annual lease. The rental price is renegotiated at the end of the lease term, and you can choose to stay and pay more, or you can move out.

You need to examine the landlord's responsibilities and your responsibilities and have a trusted friend who has rented before or an attorney look over the contract before you sign.

Deposits

A security deposit is usually required when you sign a lease. This deposit can be retained by the owner for damages made during your stay in the space or if you have to move before your lease is up. A cleaning, pet, or key deposit also may be required. These are usually refunded when you turn in your keys and the owner inspects the property. (Speaking of pets, respect the owner's rules. Don't try to sneak in Iggie the iguana if pets are not allowed.)

Renter's Insurance

You should seriously consider having renter's insurance, because it covers furniture and personal belongings, protects you from being sued by the owner's insurance company if there is damage to the property, and covers the liability if someone is hurt on the property because of your negligence (someone falls or trips over a toy and is injured). Content and liability insurance usually costs about $100 to $200 a year and is well worth it, unless you can afford to replace all your belongings and have plenty of money on hand to cover exposed liabilities.

ADDITIONAL HOUSING OPTIONS

- Become an apartment manager where your rent and all housing expenses are free in exchange for your management of the apartment complex.

- Rent space in your home to another single-parent family or single adult or a college student, and do background checks to make sure the renter is safe to be around your family. You might also enjoy having an international student, but be sure that any language barrier does not confuse the terms of your agreement.

- Look for a co-op, which is usually a condo or apartment community that is privately owned and regulated by the members who live there. Payments are based on income, so payments increase as your income increases, but each unit has an established limit to the maximum payment. There are usually long waiting lists to apply, so if you locate one you're interested in, sign up as soon as possible.

- There are programs throughout the country that help people become homeowners.[22] Check to see what's available in your area. You might find listings in the yellow pages, through your municipal government, or through the church.

- If you are overwhelmed with providing housing for your family and need help in developing life skills to manage your life, you might be eligible for Christian programs that include housing. Fees are charged instead of rent, and the organizations usually require you to take steps to improve yourself and your situation during your stay, which is typically up to two years. Fees are often reimbursed to help you move out.

- Learn to do simple home repairs yourself. Take free classes at the local home improvement store or join friends who are working on their own homes to learn skills. Purchase a few tools and learn how to use them. This takes a little confidence, which you can gain by helping others with experience do repairs in their home.

- As a last resort, if your income is very low, you can visit your local housing authority to see if you are eligible for a subsidized rental. Section 8 is one such government program. Be aware, however, that the wait for subsidized housing can be two to three years. Since the wait is so long, you would probably be a good tenant and committed to remaining in the program. The renter pays a portion of the rent, and the government pays the rest. You can find good landlords and fair locations for Section 8, but typically they are not in the best neighbor-hoods—so be careful.

 *Denise's income dropped from $45,000 a year to $21,000 a year after her divorce. Her biggest concern was having "latchkey" kids. They were teens and felt too old to have babysitters, which she couldn't afford anyway. But she also remembered being a teen, and if ever there was a time for supervision, it was then. She had already faced the fact that she was going to have to move, but hadn't found a place she could afford. Her mother offered space in their finished basement, but Denise felt that might mean an imposition on Mom. Her mother assured her that it wouldn't and she would be around to "check in" on the teens. Reluctantly, Denise moved in. She shortly found God's plan in the move when her mother answered the door for a sixteen-year-old boy who came over to watch a movie with her sixteen-year-old Kimberly! Grandma said to the boy, "What movie are we going to watch? Want popcorn?" Saving money and saving your teens—what a deal!*

AUTO

Once upon a time we would walk, hop on a donkey, or hitch the pony to a cart when we needed to go someplace. But unless you live in a city with good public transportation, the reality today is that a car is virtually a necessity.

You may be shocked at the rise in gas prices over the past few years, but believe it or not, there are many things you can to do cut down on the gas you use. If you can carpool with at least one other person for the commute to work, you've already taken a step in slashing costs. And if you plan ahead, you can combine errands and save gas instead of going to the library on Tuesday, the bank on Wednesday, and the fruit stand on Thursday. Use the most direct route.

Here are some other ways your driving habits can save you gas and money.

- Drive as though you have a cup of coffee on the dashboard—no jerky starts and stops.

- Coast up to traffic jams by lifting your foot off the gas pedal instead of approaching at full speed and slamming on the brakes.

- Use air-conditioning only when you absolutely need it. Think fresh air (unless you're in traffic and breathing fumes!).

- If you're on the highway and your car has cruise control, use it—same with overdrive.

- Fill up in the early morning or on cooler days—colder gasoline is more compact, so you'll get more drops of the precious fluid for your dollars.[23]

- As you drive at speeds over 60 mph, your gas mileage decreases. Check out fueleconomy.gov to see how driving speeds affect gas mileage.

- A great way to get a grand total of 0 miles per gallon is to idle the engine. Idling wastes about a quart of gas every fifteen minutes.[24] No more than thirty seconds of idling on a cold winter day is necessary.[25]

You Can Bank On It

"Unless the LORD builds the house, its builders labor in vain" (Psalm 127:1).

"The Lord . . . blesses the home of the righteous" (Proverbs 3:33).

"Therefore everyone who hears these words of mine and puts them into practice is like a wise man who built his house on the rock. The rain came down, the streams rose, and the winds blew and beat against that house; yet it did not fall, because it had its foundation on the rock. But everyone who hears these words of mine and does not put them into practice is like a foolish man who built his house on sand. The rain came down, the streams rose, and the winds blew and beat against that house, and it fell with a great crash" (Matthew 7:24–27).

- Keep the car cleaned out since extra weight decreases gas mileage.

- Regular gasoline is sufficient for most cars most of the time. You only need a higher grade if the manufacturer recommends premium.

- Check your tire pressure weekly. For every pound your tires are underinflated you can lose up to 6 percent in gas mileage. This means that if your tires are five pounds underinflated, you'll use up to 30 percent more gas. Check the tire pressure every week.[26]

- Don't top off (overfill) your tank when pumping gas.

 *Penny was raised in a family of boys. She did everything they did, including working on cars. She even helped rebuild an engine when she was just a teen. When she was in a two-income household she could afford to pay someone to care for her car and didn't really think about it until her income was stretched too far to pay for help. When the car needed a tune-up, she thought, I can do that and save some money. She opened the hood, feeling confident. She also thought this would be a good learning opportunity for her son Tim, who was fourteen. She removed the air filter, remembering that the carburetor was underneath it in most cars, but she couldn't find the familiar . . . what was it called? The little flappy thing on top. Where in the world was it? This wasn't right. After what seemed like thirty minutes, Tim sighed. "Mom, you need help! The cars you worked on were ancient!" A little embarrassed, she very reluctantly called her friend Ted who worked at a dealership. Penny discovered that cars had changed since she was a teen. What used to be mechanical was now electronic. Ted helped Penny and Tim with the oil change and advised her to fit tune-ups into her budget. Tim quipped, "See, I told you that they don't make things the way they did in the olden days!"*

You already know that your car needs tender loving care but like most single parents, find this is the area you put off when funds are low.

Allowing funds for auto maintenance in your spending plan will be well worth it, as good care of your car will pay off.

- Use the grade of motor oil recommended by the car's manufacturer.

- Get regular oil changes. In addition to checking your oil, be sure the mechanic checks your spark plugs, air filters, brakes and brake fluid, transmission, and power steering fluids (some auto care centers will do this as part of the service, but others need to be told you expect this to be done).

- Have your car tuned up according to the manufacturer's schedule. Keeping your car tuned up saves 6 to 20 percent in fuel.[27]

Check into local vocational and technical colleges. They often have supervised auto mechanic classes that will do routine maintenance, tune-ups, and repairs on cars for little or no cost. You might know a friend who is knowledgeable about auto maintenance who will help you with routine checks and oil changes.

You or your teenager can help by learning minor maintenance. If the car needs repairs, ask for referrals from church, friends, and family. If you find a qualified person who does it in a home garage, you may need to pay little more than parts. (The key word is "qualified," not merely well meaning.)

If your church has a free car care ministry for oil changes and safety checks, use it; that's what it's there for. If the church doesn't have one, ask the pastor or leaders if they are interested in starting one.

The cheapest car that you will ever drive is the one you own free and clear. If you already have a reliable and safe car, keep it well maintained. If your car is getting worn out and you need to replace it, prayerfully consider your options.

The cost of paying for and maintaining a car is something with which many single parents struggle. A spending plan needs to allow 12 to 15 percent for auto expenses, including payments, insurance, gas, oil, and maintenance. A car you cannot afford is a weight that you don't want or need. To avoid this mistake, make the following commitment: *I will not buy a car I cannot afford. I will not buy a car I cannot afford. I will not buy a car I cannot afford.* And another: *I will not put car repairs on a credit card.*

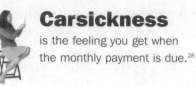

Carsickness

is the feeling you get when the monthly payment is due.[28]

New or Pre-owned?

Who doesn't like the smell of a new car? Did you know that dealers have a way of making used cars smell brand-new? There are many more cons than pros when it comes to buying a new car. For one thing, a new car loses at least 25 percent of its value in depreciation almost as soon as you drive it off the lot. The costs of insurance, registration, and licensing will almost certainly be higher, as well as taxes, depending on your state.

Most people think that they need the new car for the warranty, but that is not usually a good reason to buy one. Warranties are on the miles or years of the car and transfer to the new owner as long as the miles or years have not been met. If the manufacturer's warranty has expired, you can purchase extended warranties that cover every major part and many not-so-major parts.

Even a 0 percent loan may not justify the purchase, because the dealer is making money on the car somewhere. The only real advantage is knowing that the car has never been wrecked.

If you decide you can afford to buy a new car, consider demo cars or those that were rental cars. (Speaking from experience, I need to add that if you live in the mountains or discover the car was a rental there, make sure the brakes have been rebuilt!) You may be able to get a good deal on cars that have not sold when a new model year begins.

A late-model car or one with very few miles should be considered when you have to drive extra-long distances or you have to use your car for your job or travel.

You should buy the best car you can afford; the reality for many single parents, however, is that the cost of a new car is prohibitive.

Whether you buy a used car from a dealer or a friend or other private party, there are some things you can do to learn as much about the car as you can, such as if it has been in an accident. You can do a vehicle identification search online to find out the accident history of any vehicle you are interested in. Most dealers offer this history as well. Take a checklist to inspect the car—you can find a checklist of items that should be inspected from magazines or Internet sites. Choose your own mechanic to inspect the car.

Bring a knowledgeable person with you. Test-drive the car in various road conditions.

Ask for the car's maintenance record and find out where the car has been repaired or serviced.

The Federal Trade Commission offers this advice about buying a used car: "Before you start shopping for a car, you'll need to do some homework. Spending time now may save you serious money later. Think about your driving habits, your needs, and your budget. You can learn about car models, options, and prices by reading newspaper ads, both display and classified. There is a wealth of information about used cars on the Internet: enter 'used car' as the key words and you'll find additional information on how to buy a used car, detailed instructions for conducting a pre-purchase inspection, and ads for cars available for sale, among other information. Libraries and bookstores also have publications that compare car models, options, and costs, and offer information about frequency-of-repair records, safety tests, and mileage.

Many publications have details on the dos and don'ts of buying a used car . . .

Payment Options

If your budget is tight, you may want to consider paying cash for a less expensive car than you first had in mind.

If you decide to finance, make sure you understand the following aspects of the loan agreement before you sign any documents:

- the exact price you're paying for the vehicle;
- the amount you're financing;
- the finance charge (the dollar amount the credit will cost you);
- the APR (a measure of the cost of credit, expressed as a yearly rate);
- the number and amount of payments; and
- the total sales price (the sum of the monthly payments plus the down payment).

Used cars are sold through a variety of outlets: franchise and independent dealers, rental car companies, leasing companies, and used car superstores. You can even buy a used car on the Internet. Ask friends, relatives, and co-workers for recommendations."[29]

To Consider

Your credit score will dictate your interest rate. If you have had poor or no credit you can pay as much as 20 percent! If you have a car that is not paid off that you want to trade in, you could be rolling that amount over into a new loan and paying much more than the newer vehicle is worth, and you would take a loss if you had to sell it quickly.

If you're spending too much on auto expenses or can't afford repairs or replacement of your car, how will you handle meeting those needs?

Patience

is something you admire in the driver behind you and scorn in the one ahead.[30]

If you simply cannot afford to replace a car that can no longer be repaired, you need to pray and trust God for the answer. One single mother who could not afford to replace her car made her need known and was given four different cars from four different sources over a five-year period. The cars were older models on their "last legs," but they lasted until another came. If you're in a similar situation, ask someone to check out the car to be sure it's safe for you and your children to be in.

Auto Insurance

Your insurance agent will tell you what is required in your state to insure your car.

Liability insurance is usually one of the basics and will cover damages to any car you hit with your car if the accident is your fault. Liability will also cover injuries to persons.

If you are making payments for your car, the lender will require that you carry comprehensive coverage—for theft, damage, collision and other accidents, fire, vandalism, hail, and uninsured motorists. You may or may not choose optional features such as towing, emergency services, car rental, or loaner coverage in the event that your car is not drivable because of an accident.

Find a trustworthy insurance agent to evaluate your needs and review the suggestions below to help reduce your auto insurance costs.

- Shop around. Ask friends for recommendations, check consumer guides, and do some homework on the Internet.

- Your premium will be lower if you have a higher deductible, but if you go that route, make sure you have enough in savings for the deductible. (Some deductibles are as high as $1,000, so you'll want to have that much handy in case of an accident.) If you have a $250 deductible and switch it to $1,000, your out-of-pocket costs have gone up by $750. But if your premium is reduced, you should be able to recover that $750 in less than three years. Insurance is meant for major accidents, not for dings that we can pay for ourselves, and insurance companies prefer that you don't make a lot of small claims.[31]

- If you own a home, it's usually cheaper to have your homeowner's and auto insurance with the same company.

- Some companies offer a reduced premium for drivers who take a defensive driving course. You can always ask!

You Can
BANK On It

The Lord knows your transportation needs, just as He knows all of your needs. Be sure to seek His wisdom and leading in this important area.

■ If you're a safe driver, you should pay less for coverage. If you go for at least three years with a clean record—no more than one speeding ticket or non-injury accident—you might qualify for a lower rate.

■ If your car is worth less than $1,000, drop collision and/or comprehensive coverage.

■ Ask about discounts. Different companies offer discounts for low-mileage drivers, automatic seat belts, anti-lock brakes, air bags, good driving records, good grades for students, taking driver training courses, and so on.

■ Buy a low-profile car. Check insurance costs before you buy. Avoid thieves' favorites. Check the Internet to find out what makes of cars are most frequently stolen.

■ Some insurance companies offer lower rates for single parents with custody of their children.

■ Don't let the dog eat the homework: If you have a teen driver and her grades are good (find out how your insurer defines "good"), you can cut the cost of adding her to your policy.

GROCERIES/HOUSEHOLD

We've already set the guideline that your spending plan for groceries (include food, cleaning supplies, pet food) should come to 10 or 15 percent. To find your actual food costs, keep a detailed spending record for thirty days: include all food and nonfood products purchased at grocery stores.

Compile a list of the grocery purchases you make regularly. You'll see a list of suggested household supplies at the end of this chapter.

For those of you who love organizing lists, you can start a price diary.[32] Go through your cabinets and list food and nonedible products you buy regularly—milk, pasta, paper products, cleaning supplies, and so on. These are the items you should stock up on when they go on sale.

You can even sort these items alphabetically, by type (e.g., meat, dairy, detergent) or by location in the store.

Write down with a pencil the lowest prices you find for each item and where you bought it. When you see an item on sale, check your price diary and see if it's a good bargain. If you find the item for less, erase the higher price in your notebook and record the lower one.

Find a small notebook that fits in your purse or pocket and record your diary in it so you'll have it to consult when you shop. It'll take some effort to begin your price diary, but you'll find it's well worth it. You'll also learn to discern marketing tricks the stores use to lure you to an item on "sale." If you know how much you spent on milk last week, you'll know if this week's price is reasonable. Often stores will have a "half-price sale" one week and a "buy-one-get-one-free" sale on the same items the next week. You'll start to recognize that these items are usually being sold at the same cost.[33]

Comparison shopping is always wise, but if this kind of organizing isn't for you, you can still learn how to stretch dollars. Here are some tips:

- Prepare your own snacks: Rice Krispie treats, granola, apples, bananas, homemade cookies.

- Bakery outlet stores have a broad selection of staples and treats at wonderful prices.

- Store brands and generics are *almost* always as good as higher-priced name brands (you might find generic trash bags a little thin!).

- Keep in mind, though, that while generics are great for staples such as brown sugar, baking soda, salt, and so on, generics are not good for your pets. You'll need to keep Bowzer and Fluffy fed with quality food that provides their nutritional needs.

- Get your spices and seasonings at a dollar store, drugstore, big-box store, etc. You'll find cinnamon, nutmeg, minced onions, parsley flakes, cayenne pepper, Italian seasoning, and meat seasoning.

- Buy meat such as ground beef or tip steak on sale and freeze them. Freezer bags are economical and are generally better than freezing meat in foil.

- Plan your meals for the week so that you know exactly what you need to buy. Check the sales papers and plan your menus around what the local stores are discounting this week.

- Cook in quantity and freeze extras in serving portions to have meals for several weeks ahead. Foods that freeze well—and that kids enjoy eating—include chili, sloppy joes, home-made chicken nuggets. You can serve a leftover main dish with different sides (side dishes, that is, not a square dish with sides . . .) to create a new meal and avoid that "Aw, this again?" refrain.

- Do a quick inventory of your freezer, refrigerator, and pantry before you go shopping to make sure you don't buy something that you already have.

- Rather than buying convenience foods, such as grated cheese, prepackaged salads, or cut fruits and vegetables, prepare these at home to save a few bucks. It is always more cost effective even if your family doesn't eat it all before it expires. Most cheese freezes well.

- If time is a crucial factor some days, a product at the grocery store is always cheaper and more nutritious than at a fast-food place, so it's okay to indulge once in a while on the ready-made. And if your family members are not big salad eaters, it might be worth it sometimes to pick up a ready-made salad for one or two meals. You'll get the nutrition without wasting a head of lettuce.

- Buy in bulk when it makes sense—if you have the storage space and will actually use the items. Buying four pounds of American cheese won't save you anything if you can't eat that much and end up throwing some of it out. Warehouse shopping isn't always cheaper, but perhaps you know someone with whom you can split a bulk purchase.

- Boneless, skinless chicken breasts may cost more by the pound than pieces, but by not paying for the weight of the bones, you're usually getting a better price for your dollar than buying bone-in. This is a good time to compare. Young children, though, often prefer drumsticks.

- Look at the price cost per ounce and the serving size. A cheaper price doesn't necessarily mean you're getting a better value for your cash.

- Check the "sell by" and "use by" dates on products, especially dairy or meat products. You need to know your prices and stick to your list.

- Clip coupons if you will use them and only for items you would normally buy. Be sure to compare prices. To get extra savings, redeem the coupons on "double coupon" days. You can also combine manufacturers' coupons with store sales and in-store coupons for more savings. Some people put aside the money they save with coupons to use for a special treat.

- A little more spent on healthy choices—fresh vegetables, fruits, and grains—pays off in the end. It is no secret that too many children today are overweight. Although it's cheaper to fill up the kids with all the macaroni they can eat, be sure they're eating nutritious food.

- Shop with a list and plan your menus ahead—before you make your list.

- Plan a week's worth of meals. You might have a ground beef dish on Monday, chicken on Tuesday, pasta on Wednesday, a different ground beef meal on Thursday, grilled cheese on Friday, whatever on Saturday, chicken on Sunday.

- If you shop when you're hungry, you're more likely to buy impulsive, non-nutritious, and more expensive items. (And if you shop when you're tired or anxious, you're likely to buy items you don't need and justify it as therapy!)

- There are books and magazines that give many creative and money-saving household tips, such as using newspaper to clean windows, or vinegar and baking soda as a drain cleaner. The money you save will pay for the magazine or book in short order if you put the ideas to use.

- Watch store flyers for sales and rebates on frequently used items like shampoo, deodorant, bar soap, and detergent.

- Experiment with different stores to see what their best deals are. You might buy fresh fruits, vegetables, and meats at one store and milk and frozen vegetables at another.

- And never discount (no pun intended) the power of the dollar stores for household needs. You can dust your furniture, wipe the counter, scrub the floor, blow your nose, and put dirty clothes in items you'll find at these stores.

- Some churches or community organizations provide bulk foods from the government to low-income families. Hunks of cheese, peanut butter, and so on are available. You can contact a church or your local government to find out where these are located in your community.

- Many churches provide food at a discount to members and the community through other programs where income isn't a factor.[34]

- *And one more thing*: You've already learned how much fun it is to shop with a toddler or a preschooler. If a child is old enough, explain that you are going to the store to get certain items *only* — or you might tell him he's going to get (sugarless) gum or animal crackers on the way out. For a younger child, you might bring a special toy or trinket with you to distract her, or you might bring some kind of treat to occupy her. If you and your child are both tired, chances are she will act up and you'll react by testily giving in to whatever she wants in order to quiet her. Try to plan ahead and avoid these stressful times. This is when you remember that old adage—with children, days are long, but years are swift! But also avoid always saying no. Your child should not feel he can never have a treat. And keep an eye on that toddler. No one is slower than a toddler when you're in a hurry, but no one can climb out of a cart faster when you look away for just a second.

 *Patrick was always stressed when it came to preparing dinner for his two sons. It was so easy to go to a drive-through, but it was becoming very costly to his budget, and he knew it was not good for their health. Chasing them off the computers and game consoles and to the outdoors for activity was hard enough. He could see the boys becoming couch potatoes, with all the bulk that implies! His mother, who lived in another state, advised him to cook several*

meals once a month in order to cut down on fast food. He didn't have a clue how to do that. He didn't like cooking directions, because even when he followed them his gravy tasted like flour and his meat loaf resembled fire residue more than food. So he asked some of the women at his church. They formed a cooking club that met once a month. They bought in bulk at the warehouse store and cooked ten different dishes in one day. They divided the meals into two of each recipe per family, giving him twenty meals for the month. Eventually, the boys were convinced that their dad had learned to cook and joined in the monthly cooking events. They are grown now, and their wives are very grateful.

> ## PROFITABLE STEP

■ Choose at least one of the ideas above—such as planning a week's worth of menus and making a list or starting your price diary—and begin now!

WHEN YOU'RE STRETCHED AS FAR AS YOU CAN GO . . .

Church Aid

Maybe your food dollars just won't stretch to meet your family's needs. If you've done all you can and you still have difficulty keeping up with your family's food needs, your local church may be a good resource. Your own church might have a food pantry program and, if not, should be able to refer you to another food pantry or provide emergency funds or gift certificates from area stores for what you need.

Government Programs

I don't believe that God wants Christians to depend on welfare. I realize that we pay our taxes and expect people to be helped, but before the existence of the welfare system, families and churches took care of providing needs. We have lost much of that ideal, but things are turning around, and many caring churches have created remarkable ways of helping people, as we have mentioned.

If you are concerned because you need help and don't know what else to do, there are some biblical principles here that you can follow. As you have already learned, the first one you need to go to for help is God. He calls Himself provider and wants you to seek Him first, and He will meet your needs.

He may provide for you through your extended family. If you cannot provide all that your family needs by yourself, the first place you go for help is to your extended family. God tells us to take care of our own families, and if your extended family is able and willing to help you, you'll know that God is working through them.

If your family cannot help, you should go to the church. The Bible instructs Christians to care for the widows and orphans and those who have no one else to help them, and every church that follows biblical principles will have funds earmarked to give help with the tangible things of life to those who need it.

Food stamps and WIC are government programs to check into if you need to. Let me say again that turning to the government is not the first choice a Christian should make, but I also believe that there is no condemnation for you to take help from the government temporarily if your income is low, your need is great, and you cannot find the resources elsewhere to meet your need.

HOUSEHOLD SUPPLIES

If you know what you need and what you don't, you can save money by getting items on sale when or before you're running low. Use the following to think through what you normally use and create your own list of household supplies.

- [ ] milk
- [ ] fruit juice
- [ ] butter or margarine
- [ ] eggs
- [ ] flour
- [ ] sugar
- [ ] brown sugar
- [ ] powdered sugar
- [ ] salt
- [ ] pepper
- [ ] cooking seasonings your family likes
- [ ] baking soda
- [ ] baking powder
- [ ] cinnamon (and other baking spices)

- [ ] vanilla extract
- [ ] cooking oil
- [ ] shortening or nonstick cooking spray
- [ ] pasta (spaghetti, elbow noodles, macaroni and cheese)
- [ ] cheese (mozzarella and cheddar for cooking, slices for cheese sandwiches)
- [ ] ground beef and/or ground turkey
- [ ] round steak, tip steak
- [ ] chicken (cut up or skinless, boneless breasts)
- [ ] frozen, canned, or fresh vegetables
- [ ] baby needs

- [ ] cereal
- [ ] jelly
- [ ] peanut butter
- [ ] soups (for eating and for cooking with)
- [ ] tomato sauce, tomato paste
- [ ] beans
- [ ] pet food
- [ ] toilet paper
- [ ] tissues
- [ ] paper towels
- [ ] foil, plastic wrap, sandwich bags, freezer bags
- [ ] trash bags
- [ ] recycling items
- [ ] smoke detector
- [ ] batteries
- [ ] sponges, rags, dishcloths
- [ ] shampoo
- [ ] hair care

- [ ] bandages
- [ ] first-aid cream
- [ ] sunscreen
- [ ] insect repellant
- [ ] soap
- [ ] deodorant
- [ ] sanitary products
- [ ] cosmetics: makeup, lotion

CHAPTER 5

Getting Serious

Debt Reduction, Insurance, Childcare, Investments, Education

"The only reason a great many American families don't own an elephant is that they have never been offered an elephant for a dollar down and easy weekly payments."[35]

DEBT REDUCTION

Debt is a difficult matter. If you have debts, you already know how difficult!

There are several prominent perspectives in the Christian community as to what constitutes debt. Some say it is any note that is unsecured, such as a credit card. Others say it is anything you owe on. Still others say it is the amount that you cannot repay. It has also been said that saving is planning for tomorrow, but debt is presuming on tomorrow—presuming that you'll be able to pay your debts.

As we mentioned, debt puts you in servitude to the lender. How can anyone be sure that he or she will have the funds tomorrow to pay for something he or she wants or needs today? We don't know when our jobs will end or an illness will take us out of commission for a while. Therefore, it is reasonable to consider all loans and credit transactions debt. If you don't make your payments you will be in trouble, and the lender can collect your hide.

People sometimes believe they've gotten so far in debt that repayment is impossible, but I have seen many times over that once the individual makes an absolute commitment to pay what was legitimately due, God provides the means to do so.

As you think through your new spending plan, consider any money you've borrowed from a family member for which repayment is expected. If you have been offered money from a friend or family member to tide you over a rough time, it's best that this money be considered a gift that you are not expected to repay. Just make sure you both agree that it is a gift, and don't assume that it is! If in the future you are able to pay back the money given to you, so much the better.

Before you borrow money from a friend, decide which you need most.[36]

Likewise, you don't want to help someone else get into debt. It does not help either you or your friend to loan money when you know that he or she does not have the funds readily available to repay. It is simply best that you don't lend money to friends. If you think you should and are able to help a friend monetarily, make the cash a gift and not a loan.

Here are some ideas for getting out of debt:

- Pray. Ask God to help you become debt free.

- Follow your written spending plan. Do not accumulate any more debt.

- Destroy and close any credit cards that you cannot pay off each month. If you have more than one or one with a high interest rate, you may need to transfer them to a new card with a lower interest rate, but close the old accounts after you transfer them.

- If you feel you must have a credit card, look for one with the lowest interest rate, one that must be paid off each month or it will be closed.

- If you can, sell something and use the money to pay down a debt.

- Don't pay more than you can afford each month on debt. Many people tackle debt too aggressively, leave themselves short for the month, and consequently use more credit!

- If you can do so without depleting your savings accounts, use some of this money to reduce debt. If you're earning interest of 1 to 3 percent in a regular savings account but paying 18 percent on a credit card, you're not getting ahead.

- Beware of borrowing money to get out of debt, such as getting a consolidation loan. Your loans will be combined into one, but if you can't repay this loan, you can end up losing everything.

- Create a debt repayment plan. Pay off the smallest debt first. For example, you owe $300 with no interest to the vet and $5,000 to a credit card with 18 percent interest. Pay the minimum on the credit card and all extra resources on the vet bill. You will see immediate results in eliminating one debt.

  Put all your resources that you were paying to the vet bill on the next highest bill—the credit card, for example. You now have more resources to pay the bill more quickly.

- You may only be able to make the minimum payment due on your credit cards while you're taking care of smaller debt. But as soon as you can, add to the minimum payment. Even adding five dollars to the minimum due shows that you're working to pay down debt.

- If necessary, consider a way to generate additional income. As a single parent, however, this may not be feasible. Don't overtax yourself and leave no time or energy for your children.

- Don't make promises to pay certain amounts if you cannot keep your promise.

- If you are behind on your bills and are getting late notices, you should communicate by phone with your creditors. You might feel embarrassed, but communication is always better than silence. Most companies will work with you.

- If you are behind on debt payments and are getting collection notices, you can try writing a letter like the one below.[37] However, you may need to create a debt repayment plan with each creditor. Decide which ones to pay off first. If you need help, look for good consumer credit counseling groups that have established results in creating such plans.

Dear Sir or Madam,

I am writing to you about my account _____ . I'm sorry I have failed to abide by the terms of the agreement but am committed to full repayment.

I have limited funds available for repayment of debts, but I have received assistance in assessing my financial situation [if this is true] to determine what I can afford to pay my creditors at this time.

I am enclosing a check for _____ and will pay this amount monthly for the next _____ months. After that time I will review my situation and hope to be able to increase my payments.

If you will kindly reduce the interest rate you are charging, a greater portion of my payment can go to principal reduction.

If you are unwilling to accept my proposal, please return my check and contact me at _____.

Thanking you in advance,

(signed) _____

INSURANCE

Life Insurance

The purpose of life insurance is to provide for your children in the event of your death. Certainly this is not pleasant to think about, but one of our responsibilities as a parent is to provide today—and provide for tomorrow.

There are a few considerations for you to look at to decide how much insurance you actually need. First is the other parent's contribution. If he or she is in the picture, you may only need to provide enough for your interment.

If the other parent is not in the picture or is not able to properly care for the children's needs, you'll need to determine how much help this person or other family members may need to provide housing, food, clothing, and possibly education for your children and how long this help will be needed.

There are many variables, such as the ages of your children, your existing debts, your Social Security status, and any other sources of income your children will have upon your death.

Finally, you'll need to see how many assets you have that will be liquidated to provide care for your children. Do you have equity in a home? Furnishings? Any collectibles that will not be passed on to your children? Determine how many assets you have that will be liquidated to provide for them.

Ideally, in your absence, other family members will care for your children. (Take note: If all you have in the world is a bagful of bills and a child, *you need a will*. If you need a lawyer, get a recommendation from someone at church and look for a Christian lawyer who will draw up a simple will affordably. If the children's other parent is not in the picture or is not an option for guardianship, do not put off naming a guardian for your children.) But perhaps your parents cannot take the children, and your brother already has seven children and, while willing and glad to raise your children, will be financially stretched without the financial provision to do so.

Almost four in ten single parents have no life insurance at all.[38] If you're stretched financially, health insurance comes before life insurance, but as soon as you can afford it, a minimum policy would be worth the expense.

The two basic types of life insurance are term and permanent. Term life insurance typically offers the greatest amount of coverage for the lowest cost and provides coverage for a specific period of time. For most people, term life insurance is all they need. You can get a policy for a term between one and thirty years. Upon the death of the insured, term life insurance pays the face amount of the policy to the named beneficiary.

Whole, or permanent, life insurance provides lifelong coverage as long as the premium is paid, and accumulates a cash value that can be borrowed against. It is not a good idea, though, to consider a whole life insurance policy as a savings plan or part of your investment strategy. Remember, life insurance is to provide if you are not there.

For most single parents, a term life policy is sufficient. Monica asked, "I'm a 34-year-old single mother with three young children. I have about $225,000 in term life insurance. Should I convert to whole life insurance?" She was advised, "I don't see why you should. What you need at this point in your life is basic insurance protection, a policy that pays a death benefit that can provide income and assets for your children in the event you're not around to do that yourself."[39]

> PROFITABLE STEP

■ Decide how you're going to prepare a will and take action to do so. Also, make a list of important documents and their location and tell someone where to find them.

Disability Insurance

Although most people are not going to become permanently disabled, some do.

Check to see if you already have short- or long-term disability coverage through your employer. If you don't, consider buying your own. If your employer offers short- and long-term disability, you should be able to get it for a very reasonable cost. Health insurance will cover your medical needs, but it can't make up for lost work time in the event of an accident or medical problem that prevents you from working. A disability policy should replace 50 to 70 percent of your income if you can't work.[40] In the event that you do become disabled, you might qualify for Social Security Disability. To qualify, you must have worked in jobs covered by Social Security and have a medical condition that meets their definition of *disability*. The administration usually pays monthly cash benefits to people who are unable to work for a year or more due to a disability.[41]

Private or employer-sponsored disability insurance plans can be a source of income while a Social Security claim is pending or while a denial is being appealed.

If your employer doesn't offer this benefit or option, consider this after health insurance.

Health Insurance

If you have less-than-adequate health insurance, you know the pressures it can cause when a family member needs medical care. An accident or injury can easily rack up bills for hundreds of thousands of dollars, and you could have debts that will follow you for years.

The most cost-effective health insurance for you and your child is one where costs are greatly reduced, and that would usually be through an employer-sponsored plan.

Most companies provide a company-sponsored group health insurance plan, but most require employees to pay part of the expense for these plans. Again, you have options. You can raise your deductible and pay less. You won't have to cover the children if the other parent has them covered. You can opt out of dental if you have it budgeted and saved. You can opt out of disability at first. Talk with your plan administrator to make sure that you know your options and what you will be responsible to pay.

However, before opting out of an employer-sponsored benefits you should compare the premium cost to what you would spend if you had to cover that expense without insurance. Although you do need to pay a monthly premium, it may end up saving you thousands of dollars' worth of medical care. Most employer-sponsored medical plans have much lower deductibles than affordable independent plans.

Many employer-sponsored plans also cover preventive medical service without requiring you to pay a percentage, which can end up keeping you healthier and cost less in percentages paid for illness. If you purchase your own plan, it may not cover preventive services.

If your children are covered under their other parent's health plan, find out what benefits are available, how to process a claim, and how much of the uncovered expenses and deductibles you will have to pay. In the case of custody agreements, the document often states which parent's plan is responsible for providing health insurance for the child.

If your children are covered, you will probably be able to pay a lower monthly premium to cover only yourself.

Most major insurance companies also offer private plans for individuals who are not part of a company plan. Some Christian organizations offer programs where members share their particular medical situation and the expense is met by the other members. Be sure to research what they cover—often the program is intended as major medical coverage for hospitalizations or major medical situations and will not cover vaccinations, well-child checkups, or preventive medicine, and will have certain requirements for preexisting conditions.[42]

Saving on Medical Needs

Insurance might not cover all your medical expenses—there are deductibles, doctor and dental bills, eyeglasses, prescription drugs, orthodontist visits, and other needs that insurance does not pay. If you will have a problem meeting your part of the bill, tell the doctor your situation. He or she might be willing to provide low-cost service to low-income clients or to work out a payment plan for you.

Research health centers and doctors' offices that offer services on a sliding-scale basis, or consider a free clinic, if that is what is needed.

If you don't have dental insurance, contact a dental school and see if they offer supervised cleanings, fillings, and other work on your and your children's teeth. One family I know of had two children's teeth straightened by orthodontia students.

And if you need to, share your needs with other Christians. The church body is there to help one another along.

If you are still in need after researching these options, your local health department often offers immunizations and other services at low costs to the community. Plus, if your income is very low because you are temporarily out of work, you may qualify for government-sponsored heath care through the welfare department. This sort of assistance ends as soon as you have a job.

CHILDCARE

As a single parent, providing the best possible childcare will be a high priority. The best way to find quality, affordable care for your children is to be creative and shop around.

- You might find a stay-at-home mom who is willing and eager to earn some extra money caring for your child. An in-home arrangement will nearly always cost less than institutional day care, but not always. Be sure to make the terms and expectations clear on both sides—will the care provider need to take your child to school and/or pick her up at the end of the day? Will you leave the choice of television programs up to the provider, or do you have strong feelings about what you prefer your child be exposed to? Does the provider have a backup plan in case of emergency?

- A homeschooling family may be able to care for your children while you're at work. Some homeschoolers have children of their own who are old enough to help with the younger children, and since their school day may be completed in the morning, there will be more time to spend with your child.

- Church-based programs sometimes offer scholarships or sliding-scale fees to low-income families. If you work at the church or school, your fees may be reduced.

- Your local public school might have a state preschool program.

- Head Start, a government-based program, provides preschool for low-income families with children ages three to five.

- Start a day care business in your home. Check for local requirements and regulations. Benefits include ministry opportunities with other children, tax deductions for home businesses, and a safe environment for your children. Keep good records, save receipts, and consult with a tax adviser. Your homeowner's insurance will cover up to a certain number of children in your care in your home (be sure you're protected in case of mishap or injury to someone's child). After a certain number of children, you'll need business insurance. Check with your agent.

- Keep your children with you at home by starting a home-based business.

- Swap babysitting with a friend who has a different schedule.

- After-school programs are often provided at low cost by the local YMCA, area churches, or boys' and girls' clubs.

INVESTMENTS

This is one area you might think is never an option for you, but this is the area that will most likely help you reach some of those long-term goals. As things look today, it is unlikely that Social Security income alone will be enough for your mortgage and personal care when you are no longer able to work. Although this seems like a long time from now, it will come.

When planning for retirement, consider what is important to you.

Do you want to have enough money to enjoy a great trip? Will you want to work fewer hours without worrying about finances? Will you want to sponsor a missionary or go on short-term mission trips? Do you hope to donate to medical research or to a college? Do you just want to be able to go out to eat once in a while?

As retirement gets closer, you'll give more thought to these questions. For now, though, on those days when you feel you're simply on survival mode, give some thought to how and when you'll be able to supplement your future income through investments.

You may be eligible for investments through your employer. If your company offers a 401K or a 403B, take advantage of it. If your employer offers a matching contribution plan, sign up for it as soon as you qualify.

If you would like to invest on your own, remember that professionals who charge a fee to handle your account are the best source of advice. Be sure you can spare the funds you're using to invest.

If you have many years of working ahead of you, you'll be advised to take some high-risk investments. The lower-risk ones are for later in life when you'll be least able to take the loss. Experts say to diversify investments; i.e., invest in several different areas, not just one. Sadly, many people have put all their investment eggs into one Sure-Thing-My-Neighbor-Told-Me-About basket and have needlessly lost money.

Make sure you choose a firm and broker you can trust. You might also join a group that invests together. Costs are very reasonable, but you'll have to do your homework. Use the public library as a resource, read magazines, and look on the Internet for proven and reputable clubs.

School Days for the Kids

Many single parents dismiss the idea of sending their child to a private or Christian school because of the cost. However, many schools offer help to pay for education. One Christian elementary school has a Student Help program, but the family must ask about it. The only way to know if financial aid is available, or if your family is eligible, is to ask and then apply.

Saving for the Kids

There are some savings and investment plans designed to help parents save for their children's college education. If you will be at least 59 1/2 when your children are in college, you may invest up to $4,000 per year in a Roth IRA account.[43]

Section 529 College Savings Plans are offered by several states and are an excellent way of putting some money aside for the future. Contact the office of your state treasurer for information. You can ask grandparents, aunts, uncles, and others if they would like to invest in your children's future in this way.

School Days for You

A big part of improving yourself and enhancing your skills on the job is furthering your education. You might do this by taking training courses related to your field. Your employer will be pleased if you demonstrate interest in learning more about your business, and most companies will pay for a certain amount of training. Watch for seminars and workshops that would be helpful.

YOU CAN

BANK ON IT

"If you think education is expensive, try ignorance." [44]

With more knowledge and skills, you'll be better equipped to compete in the job market. Refine your career as you go along. Prepare to move into new areas of work that suit your individual talents and personality. Be flexible and able to adapt to change. We'll talk more about you and your job in chapter 8.

Earning a college degree might help you in your career. Often an employer has set aside funds for the continuing education of employees. If not, and if furthering your education will help you meet your career goal, there are many local scholarships, federal work-study programs, grants, and other opportunities available. Sources of financial aid are often available to help meet educational costs.

You can apply the financial aid information given here to both your education and your children's.

Financial Aid for Education

Many private, parochial, or Christian schools and most colleges have scholarship funding available for deserving students.

For college funds, you may also apply for the federal Pell grant and local state grants through the financial aid office of the school, or you can begin with the U. S. Department of Education's financial aid Web site: www.fafsa.ed.gov. You'll need last year's tax form and your Social Security number (or your child's, if you are applying for financial aid on behalf of your son or daughter). They will compute what your "expected family contribution" is based on the number of students in your family and on your income. The school(s) you indicate you're interested in will be sent the results.

Get your application in to FAFSA[45] as soon as you can. The earliest you can probably do it for a fall semester is as soon as you receive your W-2s for the previous year and fill out your tax form.

Applying for Scholarships or Grants

Private schools can be affordable, even for the single parent, if the school offers a scholarship program. Parents may be able to exchange services to help pay tuition.

A little research can help lighten your financial burden considerably if your desired job requires more education than you have or if you are sending a child to college or a tuition-based school.

You or your child could be eligible for different amounts of aid at different schools.

Grants and scholarships are not loans and do not have to be repaid. These are available directly through the educational institution. You usually have to be registered at a school before you can apply for financial aid or grants. After you register, begin by picking up forms from the financial aid office, complete all the forms, and get them in before the deadline in order to be considered to receive funds. Based on the information provided on the form, the granting institution will determine what you can afford to pay for your child's schooling. Factors considered are the family's income and the number of children in private school and college.

You will need your previous year's tax return to complete the forms, and include any extenuating circumstances that might help determine the amount of financial aid you may be eligible to receive. If you have unusual personal or financial circumstances that don't appear in the numbers but affect your family's ability to pay for education (such as high medical expenses or disability), write a letter. Explain in detail your financial situation, and note any special circumstances. Work together with your school to put together a financial package. Besides need, academic performance may be considered when granting aid, as well as special abilities (e.g., sports, music). Part of the financial aid package could include work-study.

If you search the Internet and find books from the library on the subject, you may be able to find other sources of financial aid besides the school you or your child will attend. Details are provided about the type of education or career goal that the grantor is willing to support. If you fit, you should apply. If you are awarded enough of this kind of funding, you may not need loans, and you may have extra for books and other expenses.

Most people will need to use a combination of grants and scholarships and some of the options described below in order to complete their educations. Obviously, cost will be a major criterion in selecting the right school, but you need to investigate all the possibilities before you decide you can't afford a school you really want to attend—and one that meets your educational or training goals.

There are other options for financing a college education for yourself or your child.

Your child might consider ROTC or another service program. Find out what the options are and what your child's obligations are. Another idea is Americorps (americorps.org). This program helps with college tuition in exchange for a commitment of varying length to serve with certain organizations, such as Habitat for Humanity, the Red Cross, working in a school, and so on.[46]

Many adults take advantage of degree completion programs in which you can get credit for life experiences. These programs are designed with working people in mind, and typically meet one evening a week.

Some companies offer tuition reimbursement for their employees. Another possibility for financing college is to go to work at a college. One man started working as a cook in a private college and learned that, as an employee, he was eligible to take one or two tuition-free classes each semester. He went back to college part-time and fulfilled his ambition of completing his degree, just for the cost of books and fees.

Another bonus of working for a college is that some offer free tuition to children of employees, so consider that when you're looking for work![47]

You Can Always Ask!

Is your family willing and able to help you attain your educational goals? Can they help with housing, college funds, or childcare? Can your child's extended family help him or her with further education?

Loans

Since we've talked so much about debt in this book and you don't want to incur any more, you'll need to think carefully about taking out loans to pay for a college education.

On the plus side, college will probably help you or your child attain a better-paying position after graduation. Ideally, your loan amount will be paid back in manageable payments. Still, many people find themselves with many thousands of dollars of debt from educational loans. Consider what current debts you have, and remember that school loans must be paid back. Do your best to fund education without loans.

However, if you must borrow, get the lowest student rate you can, and borrow for as short a time as possible. Pay the loan back as soon as you can, and live sacrificially in order to get out of debt.

> PROFITABLE STEP
> ■ Never stop learning! Keep your mind open and fresh. Join a
> Bible study, memorize the books of the Bible, read the newspaper,
> try a magazine other than ones you usually read, tackle a cross-
> word puzzle or Sudoku, browse in the library. See what your local
> park district offers for adults. "Instruct the wise and they will be
> wiser still; teach the righteous and they will add to their learning"
> (Proverbs 9:9 TNIV).

MISCELLANEOUS

You didn't think we wouldn't cover the most talked about category of all, did you? Miscellaneous! Here are just a few more ways to save some bucks here and there. Jot down your own, too.

■ Discount stores, discount pharmacies, or closeout stores usually offer brand name or generic equivalents at lower prices.

■ Beauty schools and barber colleges provide low-cost services.

■ If you need a babysitter and don't know who to ask, call a local high school or church and get a recommendation. (Make sure you and your children get to know the student before you leave your children with her.)

■ If you have a friend who can cut hair, see if you can trade a service in exchange for her giving your children haircuts.

■ Your family may be eligible for the reduced-cost school lunch program. Sometimes a more healthy, less fat, and less costly alternative might be packing lunches, but that depends on your area and what the kids will eat.

■ If you don't need cable, satellite TV, or the Internet, cut them or downgrade. Your children will use these less in the summer.

- Many families are discontinuing the house phone and just using cell phones. Your primary phone is considered a necessity. All others are entertainment!

- What other ways can you and your children think of to save money?

CHAPTER 6

Lightening Up

Entertainment, Home Decorating, Clothing

Katey fretted that she was not spending enough quality time with her three children. They were growing up quickly, and she just couldn't afford a vacation. Someone suggested camping, but her idea of roughing it before single parenting had been a vacation resort with indoor plumbing and air-conditioning! But determined to make memories while she could, she borrowed some camping equipment and set out for the great outdoors. The first night was terrifying. She heard sounds she hadn't known existed. She wasn't sure if she was comforting the kids or they were comforting her as they all crawled into her tent and squeezed into her once-roomy sleeping bag. Between the hard ground, the surprising night coolness, and the sense that something was getting into their tent, they finally made it through the night, only to wake up and find a frog sharing the bed with them. They jumped and screamed and laughed as they tried to capture and free the jumping, frightened frog. Years later, they still laugh about that trip.

ENTERTAINMENT AND RECREATION

"The biggest discouragement for my children and me after the divorce was the thought that there were so many things we couldn't do as a family anymore that just weren't in the budget—like movies and vacations," one single mom lamented. Actually, she found they just had to find a different way of doing things for entertainment and recreation—rethinking recreation—but not doing without it completely. You need fun times together as a family. Here are some suggestions for family fun:

- Most communities offer seasonal opportunities—outdoor concerts, fairs, historical days.

- Save your change until you have a certain amount. Use it for a take-out pizza or a fast-food supper. Many fast-food restaurants offer menu items for around a dollar. Order water instead of pop.

- See what your public library offers. There could be story hour for young children and/or a reading program with rewards for older ones. A library might also offer puppet shows and other demonstrations.

- Craft stores often offer inexpensive or free craft classes.

- Most towns have a public park system or a community center with a variety of classes and activities such as craft classes, square dancing, sports, woodworking, swimming, day camp.

- Think of others during the holidays. Get a group to sing Christmas carols at a nursing home. Bake homemade cookies or make simple crafts and offer them to your neighbors, especially those who seem lonely.

- Go to museums, festivals, and theaters; clip special offers for children from the newspaper, or join in school field trips when possible.

- Have a movie night; check out movies at no charge from the local library, or trade movies you have with another family for the evening; pop popcorn.

- Ask your church to host a family movie night. It's fun to see a movie on a large screen if your church has one, and it's fun to enjoy it with a crowd.

- You can build up your home library with quality books by taking advantage of school book clubs and offers.

- Summer camps; Christian camps are listed in denominational newsletters, local Christian newspapers, church bulletins, and national Christian magazines. Your church will know about these and promote them.

Your Night Out

You love the kids and love being with them, but sometimes you need to get out alone or with other adults.

Some families form a babysitting co-op. You can engineer this as a single parent and enlist other single parents and married couples to join.

One mother says, "The first few months in day care, I felt I could never manage to make real contact with the other parents. Everyone was in such a rush to get home. Then the center offered a parenting class at night. Nine families signed up, and we got to know another very well. By the end of the six weeks, we decided to start a babysitting co-op. It lasted for five years and was one of the richest experiences of my life. I felt comfortable leaving my daughter Judith with all of the families. For those five years, I never had to pay a sitter, and I never had to decline an invitation because I couldn't get one.

Barb was a teacher who became a Christian later in life. She had a heart for children's camp and helped countless children whose families otherwise couldn't send them spend a week of their summer at Christian camp. The campers helped earn their way by memorizing verses and helping with pancake breakfasts, spaghetti suppers, and other service projects. If your church doesn't have a camp program, enlist the help of some others and get it started!

My daughter loved her 'co-op friends' and was eager to have them 'visit' her and go to their homes."[48]

HOME DECORATING

Sarah loved Christmas and all the trimmings that went with it. She had watched her mother with delight when she decorated the family home. Somehow all the family decorations disappeared after her mother died, and Sarah had little resources to replace them. "It broke my heart that my children would not have the experience I had." One night she had a revelation about how to rebuild her collection. "I called all my relatives and asked each one to send me a favorite decoration that they thought my mother would have enjoyed. Some sent two or three! We ended up with the most beautiful and unique tree and home, and I didn't spend a dime above the long-distance calls."

Would you like to come home to a beautifully and frugally decorated home? Here are some ways to make your own "house beautiful."

- If your walls are too bare, cover them with sheet music (yes, try it), old glass plates, a quilt or cut-up and hemmed quilt pieces. And calendars are a terrific way to add art. You can buy calendars at half price for the new year on January 1, and you can find calendars with photographs you like throughout the year at remarkably cheap prices. Pick up some inexpensive frames or make your own, and you can decorate your walls with any theme, from ice cream to Ireland, from giraffes to gerbils, from classic TV shows to classical art, to planes, trains, automobiles, and more.

- You can hang many things up with poster putty, which is cheaper than frames and won't make a hole in the wall.

- A store such as Goodwill may carry new curtains, blinds, and other window treatments at far less cost than a retail store will. Go often, as the selection varies, and go as early as you can in the morning.

- Trish bought a twin sheet set and used the flat sheet to cover an old chair. She scrunched and twisted the matching fitted sheet and used it as a valance, using tacks to secure it in place.[49]

- Houseplants can add a special look to any room. Pots can be decorated with stencils, and nail polish can be used instead of paint.

- If you're artsy, you can make all sorts of interesting creations with things found in the yard, in the park, or at the beach. You can fill a vase with sand, pop in a candle, and surround the candle with shells. Use a stone as a paperweight, or drape an interestingly shaped branch with ribbon and other accessories and hang it up on the wall over the couch or over the doorway between rooms.

- If you have a place to grow flowers outside, look for sales on perennials in midsummer. They're very reasonably priced, and you'll have a head start on next year. Just be sure they're healthy before you invest in even the brightest daisy.

- If you know someone who has an abundance of hosta, phlox, columbine, or lilies of the valley, offer to thin them out of their yard and transplant them into yours. You'll be able to enjoy them this year, and they'll come up strong next year.

- Plant bulbs such as tulips, crocuses, and daffodils in the fall for a glorious harvest in the spring. Bulbs will come up for many years and are quite economical. Day lilies bloom in the summer and are also easy to care for and satisfying.

PROFITABLE STEP

If your kids are old enough, enlist them in an A-to-Z game of saving:

- ■ **A** good idea is to keep pennies in a jar.
- ■ **B**ake your own cookies.
- ■ **C**old water works to wash most clothes.
- ■ **D**on't use the washing machine until you have enough for a full load.
- ■ **E**very time you . . .

CLOTHING

When Aaron became a single parent, he found the clothing issue to be one of his greatest concerns. He had two preteen daughters who were getting more socially conscious each year. The bargain brands were no longer acceptable. And what did this dad know about gauchos or cropped pants? The girls were refusing all attempts he made to take them shopping. He needed help on how to afford chic on a budget! After conversing with a few other parents, Aaron reported he learned that "many of the discount stores are now carrying the right styles. There are acceptable fashions at great prices at consignment stores. And sometimes you just have to get a woman involved. I have a friend who took the girls shopping for their first bras!"

Providing clothing for yourself and your family is a big challenge—and gets more complicated when your children get older.

Be sure you're setting aside something each month for clothing, underwear, shoes, and socks. Stick to your determination not to charge clothing. Make this a matter of prayer, as you do every other aspect of your financial needs. If you don't carry your credit card, it will be harder to impulse buy!

If your children have grandparents or other family members who are able to help, go ahead and ask. Remember that God works through other people.

Brittany is known around church as "the bargain lady." As a single mom, she bought entire back-to-school wardrobes for less than $100 per child, including shoes. "I never pay full price for anything. I have found $100 shoes for $20 and winter coats for $10 by shopping after-season sales at major department stores. I bought a blouse my daughter loves for $2. You have to choose things your kids will wear. If not, it hangs in the closet and is a waste of money instead of a bargain! Stick to classic styles. I allow each child one 'fad' item per year so they feel a little trendy. This year my fourteen-year-old wanted a sparkly bag, but because the cost was high she had to match my contribution for it with her money. It is fun for me. It is like being on a mission or adventure. I'm really hunting." When the church decided that it wanted matching shirts for the youth for an upcoming mission trip, they went to the "bargain lady." She scored again, obtaining 40 quality shirts, with logos she ironed on herself, for less than $2 per shirt!

Elastic Stretches—So Can Money!

- Before heading to the store, write down your family members' sizes, including shoes, and needs. Your preschool son probably doesn't need another white shirt! Have this list handy whether you're going to a department store, a big-box store, a thrift shop, or a garage sale.

- Department stores put their seasonal clothes on clearance smack in the middle of that season. You might have experienced the frustration of looking for a

You Can **BANK** On It

"Therefore I tell you, do not worry about your life, what you will eat or drink; or about your body, what you will wear. Is not life more important than food, and the body more important than clothes? Look at the birds of the air; they do not sow or reap or store away in barns, and yet your heavenly Father feeds them. Are you not much more valuable than they?. . . And why do you worry about clothes? . . . your heavenly Father knows that you need them" (Matthew 6:25–26, 28, 32).

bathing suit in July or a coat in January! Watch the newspaper for sales and head for the clearance racks.

- Check labels. If it says "Dry clean only," put it back!

- If you need to dress well for work—in three-piece suits, for example—you can often find good bargains at department stores on sale. One mother found suits that were originally marked $200 on clearance for $30.

- Buy basic, classic styles you can wear through several seasons. Wear mix-and-match outfits; create a new outfit with a vest, jacket, or over-blouse.

- Waiting until after school starts to buy clothes lets you and your kids see what's "in." No child wants or needs to be out of it when it comes to appearance, especially as they get a little older. Stores usually begin their clearance sales shortly after school begins, so department stores are a good place to shop, as are thrift stores.[50]

- Buy sizes your younger children will grow into. If your daughter is a size 4 this winter, buy size 5 or 6 on clearance to put away for next winter. (You might want to do this on the quiet, though, and pull out the new clothes when they're going to be worn so they'll be new; it's more fun for the child than having something waiting around to be grown into.)

- You might also shop for shoes this way. The typical child's foot grows 1 1/2 sizes each year.[51]

- Give children a clothing allowance as soon as they are old enough. Let them know what they'll need to buy and what you'll provide.

- If you need an outfit for a special occasion, try a resale shop. People will purchase fancy clothes for their children to wear at

Easter or to a wedding, but never again, so they'll give them away. These will show up in resale or thrift stores.

- Some resale stores are consignment shops. You can bring in your own used clothing and the store will pay you a percentage of the sales. Be sure the clothes you're bringing in are clean, ironed, and in good repair.

- Thrift shops, such as Goodwill, Salvation Army, and others, are excellent places to find bargains. Clothes are often displayed by color as well as size; if you need a blue blouse, you can often see at a glance if they have one your size.

- Realize that you won't find everything you need at the thrift store each time you go. That's all right. Go again. Avoid coming home with a bagful of clothes nobody will wear just because you feel you had to buy *something* since you made the trip.

- Look over the clothing carefully. You'll want to know ahead of time if you'll need to repair a zipper, replace buttons, or mend seams.

- Go to garage sales. Have a garage sale. You might get together with several neighbors and have a larger sale, attracting more interest. Some towns and suburbs have a community-wide sale on a Saturday in the fall or spring.

- Do you like to sew? Do you have time? You can save money by making your children's Halloween costumes, pajamas, and many outfits. You can make several children's outfits by purchasing one basic pattern and putting together tops and bottoms in a variety of fabrics.

- Here's a tip: Watch the newspaper for sewing machines that were made for schools. When there is an oversupply, you can get a sturdy machine for a good price.

- People like giving clothes away to people they know. Do you know someone whose children are a little older and larger than yours? Let them know you'll be glad to take their outgrown clothes off their hands. And don't be too proud to accept clothes for yourself. Nancy benefited from a friend who "outgrew" her classy outfits!

- Buy new underwear and socks. You probably shouldn't buy shoes for your children that have been worn by someone else, since the shape will have been worn around someone else's feet. If you're lucky enough to have a friendly, old-fashioned neighborhood shoe store nearby, make your needs known and be a repeat customer. One mother bought sturdy school shoes for her four children for $30.

- Buy several pairs of socks in the same color. Then, just in case one or two get lost, you'll have plenty of replacements.

- Be generous in giving away your family's used clothes in good condition.

- Have a clothing exchange at your church twice a year. Offer to help organize it, but get a couple of others on your team. Remember, it's not only single parents who are looking for clothing bargains!

 *"When my daughter was in grade school and high school and we went shopping, I would only buy items of clothing on sale. She would get angry and call me cheap. I would explain that with the 25 percent off I was saving on the jeans, I could get her a top to go with them. She still grimaced and complained. But one day when she was a teenager I overheard her on the phone with a friend saying, 'You know, the stores really charge too much for their clothes. If they can afford to have a 25-percent-off sale, you know they are charging too much. I always buy my clothes on sale and can buy something with the*

25 percent I saved on my jeans. This way I get more clothes for the money.' I never let her know that I overheard that conversation, but it goes to show that beneath all the grumbling she understood the concept of being frugal. To this day, and she is twenty-eight, she is still frugal and is better at managing money than I ever was."

CHAPTER 7

Walking on Thin Ice

Budget Busters

The audience was hushed. The lights around the arena were turned low as the spotlight shone on the beautiful ice skater poised at the top of the steps. The music began, and she came down, one step at a time. The audience was in a mood of anticipation, knowing that they were in for a treat of a graceful performance.

Another stair down toward the ice, another lovely step of fluid motion . . . and suddenly the skater tripped and fell and skidded down onto the ice with a klutzy flop.

"Aaaawww." The audience groaned in sympathy with the skater's embarrassment. How had this happened? Surely the skater had prepared well for her program. How had she tripped up? Was there an unseen obstacle on the steps?

As it turned out, the skater's fall was part of her act—she was a comedic skater, and the audience quickly caught on and soon enjoyed her performance.

But preparing financially and then falling is not funny—it can be painful to trip over obstacles. In this chapter we'll talk about financial obstacles, how you can spot them, and how you can avoid them and have . . . smooth skating!

Since you've read this far, you are serious about taking control of your finances. But remember that habits that developed over a period of years will not be corrected in a day or a few weeks. Being aware of your weaknesses or patterns of behavior when it comes to money is a big step in walking carefully so you'll be aware of what might trip you up.

What might trip *you* up financially? We all run into snags, but different things trip up different people. Think about it for a few minutes. You might even jot down some of the first things that come to your mind.

In this chapter, we'll discuss areas that trip up many well-intentioned people.

DEBT

It is common for people of all income levels to use debt to subsidize their income, but it doesn't take long for that debt to get out of control and feel insurmountable. We can see this fact in the increase in bankruptcies. Debt is a vicious cycle. We borrow because we don't have enough for whatever we think we need, and then we can't repay because we didn't have enough in the first place.

A balanced spending plan helps in controlling debt, but you need to look at what may be causing that debt. One common error is to overlook nonmonthly expenses, such as doctor bills, family loans, bank notes, or repairs. Because you didn't plan for them, there is no money to pay for them when payments come due.

Perhaps the most difficult truth to face is that you have made purchases on credit instead of saving up for them. Now you're paying not only the cost of those items, but unwieldy finance charges on top of it. However, don't let yourself become discouraged if your debt is such that you feel you'll never get caught up. Review the steps to reduce and eliminate debt in chapter 5.

 *"Credit cards are my enemy," declares George. "I have learned my lesson, but I had to pay for it! My first credit card offer arrived as soon as I entered college. I immediately took advantage of the low-rate special, which, of course, increased after six months.*

"I met Shelly at college. After we graduated, we got married and did well financially. We worked hard and felt we deserved some extras but kept adding to the debt. After many fights over money, we divorced.

"I was shocked to learn that I was responsible for half the debt, even though I thought she did most of the charging and I made less money than she did. I was advised to file for bankruptcy, but I didn't because I was raised to pay my debts. I knew I was setting a bad example for my children, and I really did try to control my spending. I froze my cards in the freezer, only to thaw them out when the golf clubs I really wanted went on sale. I cut up cards but didn't close the accounts, so new ones came when the old ones expired.

"I finally repented of my spending ways, closed all the accounts, and promised that with God's help I would pay each one. When I did I found that God provided in some surprising ways. Today I own only one credit card, and it is the kind that has to be paid in full each month or it will be closed. I only use it when I know I have the funds and have budgeted for the item."

INCOME OR EXPENSE VARIATIONS

You might have an income that is irregular. If that's the case, your task of setting a spending plan is more challenging.

Base your plan on your average income over several low-income months. If you're starting up your spending plan during a low-income period, you can delay allocating funds for some of the variable expenses until the funds become available. Figure your variable expenses from last year and add 5 percent. Always keep your business and personal accounts separate. If you find surplus money, put it into savings.

IMPULSE BUYING

What ancient sage said, "When things get tough, the tough go shopping"?

Though humorous, this philosophy will land you right in credit card disaster! You don't even have to go far from home to go shopping these days. You can shop online or shop from the television at any time of day. It would be more accurate to say the tough *don't* go shopping, because it takes less effort to shop and spend than it does to refrain from shopping and spending. Although shopping can serve as a temporary mood lifter when you're down, the consequences to your budget won't lift your mood in the end — quite the opposite! There's a better way. The first step is to control impulse spending.

Impulse items are unnecessary purchases made on the spur of the moment. They are not in the budget. Maybe you bought something because it was on sale at a great price . . . or you or your kids were owed a treat.

Decide ahead of time how you will respond when an impulse buy is tempting. And if something really is a good deal, you might be able to "lay it away" and save the money for when you can pay in full.

And just don't take your checkbook, credit card, debit card, or more cash than you immediately need when you're out shopping. Make it hard for yourself to give in to temptation!

> ## PROFITABLE STEP

■ Determine that you'll wait a week before you buy anything that costs $25 or more, or wait a month for something that is over $50. If you still want or need the item after that time, go and get it if it fits into your budget. If you've changed your mind, you have that extra money to put away. A discipline like this is especially good for impulse items such as clothing you hadn't planned on purchasing.

"I Just Forgot . . . "

A great way to slip on the spending plan ice is to use a debit card or make a withdrawal from an ATM and forget to record it and subtract it from your checkbook balance.

Find a system that works for you to keep these records accurately! Angie has friends who throw debit card receipts away, so she thought she could too. After bouncing a few checks because she didn't really know how much she had in the bank, she decided she would have to do better. Now she puts all the receipts in her checkbook and records them as she would a check.

GIFTS

A major budget buster for many single parents is spending on gifts. Tradition encourages us to purchase a gift for nearly every occasion. Unfortunately, the net result is often a gift someone else doesn't want or need, purchased with money that was needed for something else.

Many times the cost is higher because the gift is bought at the last minute. If gifts are a part of your desired spending, budget for them and buy ahead—reasonably.

Write events and birthdays on the calendar and plan ahead. For Christmas or another holiday when there are a lot of people who will be exchanging gifts, suggest drawing names so no one is obligated to shop for too many people. Set and stick to a price limit. You won't be the only one pleased with this idea! See if the family agrees to being creative around a theme. For example, one year can be "gift cards only." Bob's family was tired of gift cards, so he suggested theme gifts around family members' home states. This turned out to be a unique Christmas, except that since most of the family had come from Wisconsin, there was a lot of cheese. Still, they had a good time!

Coupons are good for parents and children to give to each other: You can give your child a coupon for a later trip to the zoo, or your child can give you one with the promise of completing a special chore. This kind of gift continues to give after the special day and costs less than purchased gifts.

Because you want your children to feel special, you may be tempted to let some expenses go unpaid, rather than allow your children to do without, sometimes buying gifts even when it's not a special occasion. Place your desire to give to your children in God's hands; He wants to show you how. The following tips will help you give gifts that don't break your budget.

- Pray about the special day well in advance and ask God for guidance.

- Make the gift special. Don't buy the most popular or expensive item just because it is popular, and don't buy on the spur of the moment. Instead, choose an item your child has desired consistently for a long time. The late Fred Rogers (of *Mister Rogers' Neighborhood*) used to say that you should get the child the first and second items on the wish list and forget the rest.

- Tell your child to ask God if he or she should have it. Avoid saying you can't buy something because you don't have the money. Avoid thinking it too. God has a way of supplying anything if He wants your child to have it.

- Start saving any extra money that comes in and add one or two dollars a week toward the item.

- When you have enough, watch for the item to go on sale and buy it, even if the event is still six months away. Look at stores that have layaway plans (they do still exist).

- Saying thanks to teachers: Donate a book to the local or school library in the names of the teachers or aides who worked with your child throughout the year. Write each of them a note telling them about your donation.

- Start a houseplant in an inexpensive mug or cup.[52]

One single mother multitasked by finding a way to clean out closets and make some money to spend on Christmas gifts. She and her children went through everything that they no longer used, or wanted, or clothes that didn't fit. She gave away some of the items but stored the rest. She said, "I spent some time on the computer educating myself about e-bay. I set up my account, photographed the items in my discard pile, and set about marketing them. I soon learned that items I no longer had use for were of great interest to others, and the selling began. I am pleased to say that everything sold! I used that money to fund the gifts that I purchased for my children. Money from toys they no longer used was put into items they wished for! Without one penny out of our budget I funded their holiday."[53]

Gift giving for a parent is problematic for young children. Many single parents do not receive gifts on their special days because of this. Giving the child money to buy yourself a gift doesn't feel right, and the child still may not have someone to take him or her shopping. The following suggestions will help.

- Look for churches, organizations, or stores in your community that provide "Secret Santa" type opportunities. Inexpensive items are arranged in a special room where workers help children select gifts while parents wait outside. Gift wrapping is usually included.

- Through schools, scouts, churches, and other organizations, children often have the opportunity to make gifts for their parents. These gifts can be special treasures.

- If the other parent is not available or willing to take the child shopping for the custodial parent, perhaps friends or church members would be willing to take the child shopping.

DOWNGRADE IN LIFESTYLE

Change is hard. Typically, the family income drops considerably after a separation, and it almost always requires a lifestyle change. Some things you used to do or spend money on have to go. The sooner you accept the realities, the fewer mistakes you'll make and the less debt you'll have. The following steps will help you begin the process.

- Prayerfully consider why you think you need to maintain the same level of spending in each area. Look at the emotional reasons first.

- Ask a trusted friend to evaluate your situation with you. You need the feedback from another perspective.

- Gather ideas for cutting expenses; look at the money-saving suggestions for each category in this book. Would those cuts allow you to live within your income?

- If a major decision is necessary after doing all you can to make adjustments, make the decisions quickly before increasing debt.

- For widows and widowers: It is best to refrain from major changes during the first year after the loss of a spouse. Your decisions will most likely be made from grief instead of from a realistic financial picture. Make cuts where you can while avoiding major changes, such as selling the home, spending the insurance, or cashing in investments.

Major life changes can include moving to a smaller home or an apartment, trading in the car, and/or destroying all credit cards. Acknowledging the fact that you can't have the same lifestyle you once had is difficult, but accepting and adjusting to the limitations will make the process of financial recovery a growth experience for you and your children.

It's also a good idea to seek counsel from other people such as a budget coach, pastor, family, or friends. You might find an accountability partner, someone with whom you can share victories, frustrations, and challenges.

You might seek out an agency that offers parents an online way to share financial, social, scheduling, and parenting issues in a nonthreatening environment.[54]

Payday Loans/Car Title Loans

Avoid these temptations to quickly get money in your pocket. They'll charge an exorbitant rate of interest, and you'll find yourself more behind than before. You might even lose your car.

HOME EQUITY LOANS

You don't want to take out a loan based on the value of your house. If you can't pay back this loan, you can lose your house.

SCAMS

Although new scams crop up every day, the following list should help you learn to recognize a scam when you see one.

Prize Offers

This is an old scheme in which victims are led to believe, by phone, e-mail, or postcard, that they have won a major prize (a car, a television, a vacation, or $10,000, for example), and to receive it they have to send so much money to pay redemption fees or taxes. No one receives the prize. Remember that offers that require you to send money to activate the offer are not legitimate.

Advance-fee Loans

People with bad credit and who can't get a loan from the bank are prime candidates for this scam. Often solicited by phone or through advertisement in a local newspaper, you are assured a loan if you pay $200 or $300 in advance, as a processing fee. However, once you've paid the "advance," there is no loan.

Free Vacations

You receive a postcard congratulating you for being "approved" to receive a vacation at a resort. You are instructed to "call to confirm

YOU CAN **BANK** ON IT

There is always something—a scheme, a fast-talker, a great offer. Who said, "If it's too good to be true, it probably is"? Remember that the Lord is on your side to help you be a good steward and learn to recognize the Enemy, who "prowls around like a roaring lion looking for someone to devour" (1 Peter 5:8).

within 48 hours or you'll lose your chance." Having not been able to afford a vacation for several years, you jump at the offer. When you call, you are asked to pay a nonrefundable $50 fee to receive your "vacation certificate." After writing and mailing the $50 check, you are informed only days before the departure date that the trip was canceled, the firm making the offer had closed, and you are not only $50 poorer, but very disappointed.

Repair Rip-Offs

This scam may involve anything from offers to repair roofs, driveways, and furnaces to fixing cracked foundations. It goes like this: A truck pulls up and the driver says, "We've been repairing roofs in this area and have some materials left over. I see your roof could use some work, and since we're in the neighborhood anyway, we could do it today for half price — only $500." This tactic is often used on the elderly, but anyone is susceptible. You think you are getting a real bargain price to get your roof repaired, so you write the check, have the work done (sometimes), and the first time it rains, the roof leaks or tar washes down the sides of the house. Of course, the "repair" person has left town by then (he cashed the check only minutes after leaving your house). You now have to pay a second person to come and repair the roof and clean the tar off.

Charity Cons

Be wary of people calling for donations for charity over the phone. One scam involved prisoners calling from jail to raise money for a "policeman's charity." The unsuspecting victims not only gave funds, but revealed personal information to these prisoners. Again, never give out personal information such as credit card numbers or your Social Security number.

Secured Credit Cards

If you are offered a credit card with the stipulation of paying the processing fee of $50 or more, you are likely to be denied a card unless you can post a savings account to establish collateral. Some legitimate banks issue such secured credit cards, but avoid the independent marketing firms that charge a fee for processing (who often promise to return it if you are denied a card). Usually the victim is denied a card but, by being unable to secure the card with a savings account, also loses the $50 processing fee.

Identity Theft

No matter what kind of offer you're hearing from the nice, caring person who phoned you, *never* give out your credit card number or your Social Security number over the phone. *Never.* It's a different matter if you initiate a call to your bank or other institution. But if someone unknown initiates a call to you, do not give out any information. Hang up. Don't even give out your name, address, or mother's maiden name. You'll be surprised at how many people will ask you for your phone number when they've just phoned you.

And here's a bonus tip: Don't have your Social Security number printed on your checks.

Do not give information over the Internet unless you have initiated the contact and it's a legitimate business with a secure Web site.

Do not even reply to e-mails that request information. Hitting "reply" legitimizes your e-mail address and invites even more spam.

Do not give personal information to anyone who calls you asking for it, regardless of whether they mention a company or organization with which you do business. Ask them to send you something in writing to consider.

Do not fall for sympathy e-mails requesting help to save someone's health or life. You can Google urban legends to see if this plea has already been debunked. However, there are most likely many worthy people in your own community who could use help.

THE "THERE'S NEVER ENOUGH" MENTALITY

"Whoever loves money never has money enough; whoever loves wealth is never satisfied with his income" (Ecclesiastes 5:10).

We as adults struggle with wanting more. It can be even harder for children. They are bombarded with ads and peer pressure to have whatever's hot at the moment. They want what other children have.

If you are a single parent because of divorce, determine early on not to try to one-up your former spouse by being the "fun" parent who provides toys and outings while the other struggles to make school lunches and pay the phone bill. Children can be manipulative, even pitting one parent against the other in an attempt to get one to give in to their desires.

 "Do not value money for any more nor any less than its worth; it is a good servant but a bad master."[55]

But it's not just the children who need to learn contentment—it's us too. Who among us doesn't want to be able to give to our children the things we see other parents giving to theirs?

You don't need to overindulge with material things to make up for being a single parent. One mother said, "As a single parent I was tempted to try to show my love for my children with money. I believed that they deserved the best of everything and that with the latest widget on the market they would feel important, cherished, and valued. The reality is that children don't equate love with money. Children feel loved when we cherish them emotionally . . . and, most importantly, spend time with them."[56]

It's a hard lesson to learn, but if we can exhibit contentment, we'll go a long way in sharing with our children that the most important things in life are those money can't buy. The flip side of this reality, though, is making children feel they can never have a treat, or you can never do something just for fun. Keep in mind Proverbs 30:8–9: "Give me neither poverty nor riches! Give me just enough to satisfy my needs! For if I grow rich, I may become content without God. And if I am too poor, I may steal, and thus insult God's holy name" (TLB).

The Unexpected

"I knew that child support was not going to last forever," Jen said. "But that day came much quicker than I imagined!" When she had just gotten her youngest, Sean, off to college, the last check came. "I used the child support as income when I applied for the notes for my house and my car and always thought I would be making more money by the time it stopped, but it didn't work out that way. I lost $460 a month, without funds to cover it. It was many hot dogs later that Sean graduated. I tell other single parents to consider the support 'extra' for buying clothes for the kids or buying things you need to replace, but don't depend on it for your basic needs because you never know when it might not be there. A friend of mine lost child support when her ex changed jobs, and it was never recovered." Jen's hard sacrifice paid off when Sean went on to become a medical doctor and bought his mom a car!

The day Karen received a phone call from her daughter's caregiver saying that Cathy had gotten cut on glass and needed stitches was the same day the car hadn't started and the dryer left the clothes wet. None of us can anticipate everything that might happen, but we need to be as prepared as possible so our spending plan won't derail.

It's wise to set something aside each month for repairs and emergencies. Having these funds in your savings account will give you some peace of mind, as well as give you some cash to take care of the emergency.

And besides having some cash on hand, it's helpful to have a repair service or mechanic on hand. If you know ahead of time whom you can call when something happens, you'll tend to make wiser choices than you would by randomly thumbing through the phone book. Anticipate the emergencies and unexpected expenses, and you will eliminate a great deal of stress when they do occur.

■ Think now about whom can you turn to—family, neighbors, church—in case of an emergency. Have a backup for childcare; find someone who could care for your children in case of illness or emergency.

BEING HONEST AS ABE

There is a story of a young executive who was invited out to lunch by the owner of the company. The successful young man was ready for a promotion. When the owner took him to a cafeteria-style restaurant for the meal, he noticed that this man hid a pat of butter under a dinner roll so he wouldn't be charged for it.

Instead of promoting the executive, the owner fired him.[57]

The point of this story is to remind all of us that cutting corners and being less than upright in even the smallest of matters will not help us get ahead, nor will it secure God's blessing on our lives.

SHARING EXPENSES

You might have a roommate with whom you share housing and expenses. That's great—as long as your roommate is also a believer. "Do not be yoked together with unbelievers," we are admonished in Scripture (2 Corinthians 6:14). This verse is usually cited for a marriage relationship, but the principle stands in a housing partnership.

And be sure your roommate isn't a member of the opposite sex! Some single parents, even professing Christians, get involved in a relationship that they shouldn't be in for the sake of having someone to share living expenses. It might be tempting if you're stuck in survival mode and the opportunity presents itself. Some even justify living together outside of marriage by declaring, "God led me to him, so it must be what He wants." God will never lead you anywhere that is contrary to His nature and His will as spelled out in Scripture.

Seeking Ungodly Advice

When you do need counsel, ask. Just be sure to ask the right people. We live in an age in which we are soaked with information. As you know, you can get in front of your computer and Google nearly any subject, and you'll find all sorts of links to data, reliable or otherwise. Only consult or counsel with godly people who have a high regard for the Lord. Do not take advice, financial or otherwise, from anyone else, and certainly do not consult any sort of medium or fortune-teller or even read a horoscope.

Trying to Do It Alone

You are doing a job that was meant for two people, and from time to time you will need help. Everyone needs some kind of help sometimes, even those you think wouldn't need help now and then . . . people in two-income households, the wealthy woman down the street . . . everyone.

You would willingly help someone else if you could, wouldn't you? It might be embarrassing for you to have to ask for financial help, but remember that others are just as willing to help you as you will be when you have an opportunity to help. Don't let pride get in your way.

After church one Sunday, an older gentleman named Richard surprised Joyce with an envelope that contained a hundred dollars. He told her to use it for anything she and her children needed, and someday when she was able, she could do the same for someone else. Joyce was flustered and didn't want to accept the money, but Richard insisted.

When Joyce confided to a friend that she felt uncomfortable with the gift, her friend said, "Don't rob Richard of the blessing he has in giving to you."

To be frank, some people won't ask for help because they have asked before and were refused. They don't want to face rejection again or be made to feel like beggars. But remember that God has promised to meet our needs, and that in most instances He uses people to whom He has given a surplus to help others less fortunate. As the Bible says,

"Suppose a brother or sister is without clothes and daily food. If one of you says to him, 'Go, I wish you well; keep warm and well fed,' but does nothing about his physical needs, what good is it?" (James 2:15–16).

The following are some guidelines for ways to ask for help.

- Believe that God wants to meet your needs and that He uses others to meet needs.

- In most cases, you'll go to the pastor with your need. He will know the proper channels to follow to give you the best and confidential help for your situation. If you prefer not to take your need to the pastor, or if the church is large and that's not an option, you can call the church office. Some churches make it known whom to approach for certain needs; some churches even have an information booth. That's what the church is there for. If the church provides financial counseling, take it.

- Be willing to receive what God wants to provide.

- Be sure you are spending the money you have wisely, and willingly be accountable.

- Be willing to give as well as receive.

Okay, you've looked at your goals, assessed where you are, and looked at how you might make adjustments. You are on your way to a working budget. Now let's look at how God uniquely made you and explore other ways to enhance your opportunities to improve your situation.

PART 3

Purpose

CHAPTER 8

Made in God's Image

Your Personality and Purpose

Jessie is a list person. She likes to make a list of everything she needs to do each day, and has even been known to write, "Make a list." She finds satisfaction in scratching off items she has completed.

But one day, she felt like she wasn't getting anywhere. Her lists just itemized the same dreary routine: Get the kids ready for school, start laundry, pick up a newspaper on the way to work, go to work, work, make supper, eat supper, do supper dishes, wash more laundry, dry laundry, put away laundry, make lunches for tomorrow.

Although she was accomplishing things, her list was boring. To pep up her list she might have added bathing the dog!

What was it all for? Was there any point to it all besides getting through the day? Jessie needed a big-picture reason for the cycle of working, caring for the family and house, and making lists.

Now that you've taken the challenge of looking at your own financial situation and working it to be the best it can be, let's take a look at what your bigger picture is. In a previous chapter, we talked about setting financial goals, but without an income, there's nothing to budget to achieve these goals.

Since your income usually comes from your work, let's look at how you can see your work as more than just a way to bring in cash for daily life—work is God-given, it's important, and it's something to which you bring your own uniqueness.

Some of the questions you considered in the first chapter were:

- What character traits do I value and want to develop in my life and the lives of my children?

- Are my financial goals in line with these traits? For example, is being generous a trait I want my children to acquire?

We've been talking about a lot of planning and implementing, and by this time you might feel you've worked hard enough. After all, when you're on your own, you know that the next shift is never coming in, since when you come home from work, you'll still be working! "As a single parent, you're on overload all the time."[58]

But even though it all sounds overwhelming—and let's face it, some days it is!—it helps to keep the end in front of you; that is, the reason you're persisting, the goals you want to and *will* achieve.

MAKING THE BEST CAREER DECISIONS

This is a good time to determine your purpose in working. Certainly the most basic need is to provide for yourself and your family. Let's take a look, then, at determining what your life goals are and what your finances have to do with them. One way to do this is to develop a personal mission statement. Many large companies have corporate mission statements, smaller organizations have them, churches have mission statements; and individuals also should have a well-thought out mission statement based on beliefs, values, and goals.

A mission statement defines who you are and how that affects what's important for you to accomplish. Stating what is important to you keeps you on track and on purpose. It would be impossible to create a mission without praying and examining what God wants to accomplish through you and your household.

One writer speaks of developing a personal mission statement. He says if it is "based on correct principles [it] . . . becomes a personal constitution, the basis for making major, life-directing decisions, the basis for making daily decisions in the midst of the circumstances and emotions that affect our lives."[59] In other words, God validates who you are. He gives you purpose, values, personality, and skills to accomplish what He wants to do through you. A personal mission statement nails these down. You can measure both major and daily decisions on the basis of what you have determined to be your personal mission.

A personal mission statement will reflect your core values, your desired character traits, and contributions you would like to make in your various roles. That is, "it focuses on what you want to be (character) and to do (contributions and achievements) and on the values or principles upon which being and doing are based."[60]

Forming a personal mission statement will not only help you find a job or career path that is right for you, but it will help you see your work as part of the greater context in your life. There are different types of personal mission statements. Some people like to be very specific, and others prefer being less precise.

The following insights for developing your own personal mission statement come from Randall S. Hansen, "The Five-Step Plan for Creating Personal Mission Statements."[61]

Step 1: *Identify Past Successes.*

Think of several times over the past few years when you have been successful, personally or professionally. Some examples could be having worked on a fund-raiser for your child's school or developing new features for an existing product.

Step 2: *Identify Core Values.*

Develop a list of attributes that you feel identify your personality and your values. For example, you might be hardworking, creative, outgoing, compassionate, a good decision maker.

Step 3: *Identify Contributions.*

How can you best contribute to society in general, your family, your employer, your community, your friends? Others? Think of the various roles you already fill.

Step 4: *Identify Goals.*

List personal goals, both short- and long-term.

Step 5: *Write Your Mission Statement.*

A personal mission statement can be as long and as detailed as you want it to be, but it should give you something attainable to work with. Also, because circumstances change and you'll go from one season of life to another, make it a point to review your statement at least once a year. You might want to revise it, and you may be encouraged at how well you're doing in achieving your goals and purpose.

This person's personal mission statement reflects general traits he intends to attain:

"Be loyal. Be honest. Be compassionate. I must give respect before I demand it. I must continue to learn and grow through my entire life. I must take the strengths of my loved ones and improve on my weaknesses. Allow myself to empathize, not sympathize. Set, and follow, a good example for my family. Review my actions each and every day. Learn from my mistakes. Put faith in the Lord; in Him anything is possible."[62]

Here are some more examples of personal mission statements from single parents; their statements identify more specific values and goals:

- I need to have as much time with my children as possible in my role as their parent. Therefore, I will find a job that will enable me to keep regular hours so I will have optimal time with my children and be able to support us. I might want to find a job with opportunity for advancement, but for the next few years, my priority is to be at home when they are home as much as possible.

- I will be a dependable employee; I want to have a reputation for dependability and kindness. I will not gossip or listen to gossip. I will not cut corners in my work or have any hint of dishonesty. I will have excellent attendance. I will see an improvement in my performance review. I will make a new friend at work.

- I want to think beyond my role in the home to my role in the community, and I want to teach my children by example to care about others. To achieve this, I will find a way to volunteer in my community.

- It's important to me to keep learning. I need to improve my knowledge in the area of _____. To accomplish this goal I will read _____ magazine and try out three ideas in the next year.

- Being a parent is my most important role. I will sit down with my child every evening, even when I am tired or busy with chores, and read a story together. I will go over my child's homework each day. I will play a game with my child at least three days a week.

- I want to seek first the kingdom of God and His righteousness. One aspect of "seeking" means that my children and I will be part of a church and be faithful in attendance. I will not lie and will teach my children to always tell the truth. We will be generous and will take care of our clothes and other possessions so when we can no longer use them we can give them away for others to have.

Now that you've given some thought to what is important to you—that is, what your purpose is—what kind of values you want to have, and what you'll want to pass on to your children, let's look at how these relate to your work.

PROFITABLE STEP

- "Whatever you do, do it all for the glory of God" (1 Corinthians 10:31).

If you love your job, you already have a fit with your passion and purpose. But perhaps you don't have that sense of satisfaction that your current position is a good fit. It may be time to move into a different direction. After all, it is a God-given gift to enjoy your work. See Ecclesiastes 5:19: "to accept [one's] lot and be happy in (one's) work—this is a gift of God."

The movie *Chariots of Fire* told the story of Olympic runner Eric Liddell, who said, "God made me fast, and when I run, I feel His pleasure."

Or suppose that you have not worked, outside of caring for your family, for a very long time, and suddenly you find yourself the designated breadwinner, facing how you are going to earn a living. Where do you begin? Maybe your confidence isn't where it needs to be.

You Can

BANK On It

God has created you on purpose, with a unique personality, with talents and skills that come from Him.

You have used your skills, abilities, talents, and values to maintain that home and care for your family, and those are all transferable skills. You may have volunteered, possibly in leadership positions, and these skills can also transfer into skills you can use in a paid position. You may need some help with creating a résumé that reflects your abilities. Beyond these skills you have developed, there are God-given attributes that add to your confidence and make you desirable to employers or clients.

David sang to the Lord, "For you created my inmost being; you knit me together in my mother's womb. I praise you because I am fearfully and wonderfully made; your works are wonderful, I know that full well" (Psalm 139:13–14).

Read these verses. Read them again. Work on memorizing them so you can internalize this truth. You might be surprised to know how many people struggle with believing that God knows them personally. He made a wonderful work when He made you!

As you read through the following Scripture passages and thoughts, take the time to read these slowly. The truth underlying these simple words will carry you a long way in your walk with Christ—and in your pursuit of finding the best fit jobwise.

You have been given unique talents.

"We have different gifts, according to the grace given us" (Romans 12:6).

"The body is not made up of one part but of many. If the foot should say, 'Because I am not a hand, I do not belong to the body,' it would not for that reason cease to be part of the body. And if the ear should say, 'Because I am not an eye, I do not belong to the body,' it would not for that reason cease to be part of the body. If the whole body were an eye, where would the sense of hearing be?" (1 Corinthians 12:14–17).

Paul is humorously using the analogy of the body to show us that we all have a vital part in God's kingdom. While Paul is specifically talking about our part in the church, the point remains that God gave each of us unique talents to use—not waste. God has designed each of us with talents and gifts for His service, wherever we are and whatever we are doing.

In *Joy at Work*, Dennis Bakke says, "Isn't it logical that all work that results in food, clothing, shelter, rest or recreation, beauty, and a host of other worthy ends can be acts of worship to God and seen as valuable contributions to society? Are these not activities that can be as sacred as rearing children, teaching school, or even carrying out priestly duties?"[6] Not only have you been uniquely created with certain skills; those skills are important.

Work is important for itself, and your unique skills are important for what you bring to it.

All different kinds of work are important, because so many people have roles that are necessary to society. Do you need your washer repaired? Do you want your newspaper delivered? Do you need information about your insurance policy? Do you need to change the time of your dental appointment? People who provide these services are needed. As Bakke says, "Humankind's first important job description was to manage the Earth and all that comes from God's creation. I believe this includes the ideas, services, and products that come from the imaginations of people."[64]

You must develop these talents and strive for excellence.

"Do you see a man skilled in his work? He will serve before kings; he will not serve before obscure men" (Proverbs 22:29).

When God gave instructions for constructing the tabernacle in Exodus 36, He looked for skilled workers: "every skilled person to whom the LORD has given skill and ability to know how to carry out all the work . . ." (v.1); "every skilled person to whom the LORD had given ability and who was willing to come and do the work" (v. 2); "skilled craftsmen" (v. 4); "all the skilled men (and) skilled craftsman" (v. 8). "Every skilled woman spun with her hands and brought what she had spun" (35:25).

"It's good to have money and the things that money can buy, but it's good, too, to check up once in a while and make sure that you haven't lost the things that money can't buy."[65]

Every aspect of building and even decorating—adding beauty to—the tabernacle was important to the Lord, and He valued skill and excellence. You don't want to present less to Him in whatever work you do. You should do your work as if you are actually working for the Lord, because you are. "And whatever you do, whether in word or deed, do it all in the name of the Lord Jesus, giving thanks to God the Father through him" (Colossians 3:17). Using your God-given talents to their fullest will give you success and joy.

Using your talents in work is a form of worship to Him.

As the author of *Joy at Work* says, "We honor God by furthering His creation. Work should be an act of worship to God. God is pleased when people steward their talents and energy to achieve these ends."[66]

And, as Jesus said, "Let your light shine before men in such a way that they may see your good works, and glorify your Father who is in heaven" (Matthew 5:16 NASB). When you let your light shine, others will see Christ through you. Work is an excellent place to be a witness for Him, both in your approach to your work and relationally to those with whom you come in contact.

> ### PROFITABLE STEPS

■ Seek God's direction and confirmation as you explore various occupations and careers.

■ Write your personal mission statement and perhaps a family mission statement.

■ Keep it in a place you'll look at often—in your Bible, on the bathroom mirror

----

WHAT KIND OF FIT IS BEST?

As mentioned, you may already be in a job that suits you. Or it might be time for a change. God may be moving you in a new direction.

If you believe you need a shift in your job situation, there are several things to consider. You don't want to make any change hastily; be prepared for any time between jobs without income. Be sure you have a new job lined up before leaving your current one.

■ What kind of work are your God-given personality and talents best tailored to?

■ Do you like working with people, or do you like working alone?

■ Would you rather be part of a team project or be responsible for something by yourself?

■ Do you enjoy working with the public? (i.e., are you suited to be a server in a restaurant, a salesclerk, receptionist, etc.?)

■ Do you mind driving on the job? (e.g., picking patients up for medical treatment)

- Do you like working with your hands?

- Do you like routine? or are you more spontaneous?

- Do you like working with children?

- Do you have ambition to move up? or at this time of your life are you content to have a job that allows you to be home most of the time your children are?

Nancy Sebastian Meyer, author and certified personality trainer, created these thoughtful questions that will help you find your "inner core of uniqueness." She says, "Answer these questions in light of a work environment. You may find yourself in the middle of some of these questions, not at one extreme or the other—which is totally fine, too! There are no 'right' or 'wrong' answers, simply differences."

- Are you people oriented or project driven?

- Do you consider yourself more of a leader or a follower?

- Are you more factual or imaginative?

- Do you tend to "just get it done," or do you follow steps and enjoy lists?

- Do you look more for the "big picture" or need details?

- Do you tend to "think out loud," or do you process thoughts internally?

- Are you a quick thinker or are you patiently prudent?

- Do you ask for help or enjoy figuring out a problem by yourself?

- Which describes your general outlook: optimistic, realistic, or pessimistic?

- Do you like to use a schedule or "go with the flow"?

- Do you enjoy a quiet, peaceful, or high-energy, loud, busy atmosphere?

- Do deadlines make you work more efficiently or make you nervous?
- Would you say you need more fun or seriousness in your workplace?
- Are you a "mover-shaker" or a low-energy person?
- Do you enjoy leadership, or would you rather be a follower?
- Do you work best in an organized or cluttered environment?
- Do you work better by yourself or on a team with one or more other people?
- Is it easy or difficult for you to remember details?
- Do you consider yourself to be powerful, popular, peaceful, or perfectionistic?
- Are you easygoing or intense?
- Do you need frequent verbal encouragement or occasional significant recognition?
- Do you work better with just one other person or a group?
- Are you an influencer or encourager?
- Do you tend to be more intentional or spontaneous?
- Do you say "it is what it is" or "it's not always what it seems"?
- Are you self-motivated, or do you need encouragement from others?
- Are you a better listener or talker?
- Do you generally read the directions or just follow your instincts?
- Would you rather be told or shown?
- Are you more detail oriented or relationship oriented?
- Are you an originally creative person or one who enjoys editing and manipulating what has already been given?
- Do you recharge on people or alone time?

- Where are your greatest skills and interests: words, people, vision, organization, logic, humor, creativity, or physical activity?
- Do you try to live within the letter of the law or tend to rebel against authority?
- Do you have a positive or negative self-image?
- Are you a risk taker, or do you play it safe?
- Do you like to work with your hands, your mind, or people?[67]

For another activity concerning your personality, you can go to www.crown.org, Tools, and click on Personality ID, an interactive assessment tool.

WORKING FROM HOME

Employers are looking for ways to save overhead costs, and many are paying employees who work from home. Some people are employed by others but can operate from home, with the availability of a computer, fax, high-speed Internet, e-mail, and access to the company from home. In what ways would your working from home help your boss, such as in office space or equipment? If you can offer suggestions, your employer might allow you to work more from home.

If you already have a job and can spare the time, you might supplement your income with a part-time home business.

One mother came up with an inexpensive way to make a little extra money. She made beanbags. She designed them in the shape of frogs and filled them with birdseed, making them more flexible and not so lumpy as beans. She sold them at craft shows, displaying them in different poses. She kept her costs low by making the frogs from fabric remnants.

Matthew Osborne stepped right into a way to make extra money— he started a business removing dog waste from their owners' yards. This entrepreneur from Columbus, Ohio, continued to make money from his highly successful business even after he sold it by writing a booklet that he sold on the Internet—a booklet about starting a pet waste removal business![68]

Ask yourself if you have a hobby that can be turned into a home business. You might or might not find a source of income that would equal that of a full-time job, but you can supplement your income in many ways.

If you have good typing and writing skills, you can make extra money typing term or research papers, correspondence, reports, and so on. You can provide a service writing résumés, sending out bulk mailings, doing or medical or legal transcription. If you are creative and good with graphics, you can write newsletters, brochures, flyers, and business cards.

One person was skilled as a mechanic and built a business doing car repairs. But he set up his van with tools and auto parts and went to the customers so they wouldn't have to take time to drop their cars off at a shop.

Do you have a service to offer that you can take to clients?

If you've been in the business world and have some knowledge of such things as sales, computers, self-defense, etiquette in the office, etc., you can create a training presentation and sell it to corporations. Contact a company you're interested in and ask for the training department. If they don't have one, start with human resources and explain what you want to do. When you give a presentation, be sure to provide your business cards or a flyer of your services.

Here are some other ideas: Can you decorate cakes? Refinish furniture? Tutor? Write for the neighborhood newspaper? Paint or wallpaper? Clean houses or a church? Be a clown at children's parties? Cook for a caterer? Make crafts to sell? Give music lessons? Phone people on behalf of AMVETS or Purple Heart to see if they have donations to be picked up? Teach aerobics or another class at the community center? Be a photographer at a wedding or other special event? Do specialty sewing such as sewing emblems on uniforms?

Many people earn income by selling products at home parties. You can present and sell home decorating items, baskets, makeup, glassware, cooking utensils, jewelry, artwork, and chewing gum (okay, maybe not that last one, but you get the idea).

If you're available at different times of the day, you can be a mystery shopper. A company will hire you to be a customer who's shopping for anything from a mattress to hardware or who's a patron at a restaurant. The mystery shopper reports on the quality of service. You won't be paid a lot, but you'll make a little money and might get lunch at a nice restaurant.

Your child or teen can feed the neighbor's cat and clean the litter box when the neighbor goes on vacation. Running errands for an older person or a busy person is another service your kids can do.

Maybe your goal is to become self-employed full time. It takes two to three years to establish enough business at home to quit your day-time job, but that shouldn't stop you if you have the persistence to see it grow. Just be creative.

With the savings in childcare, transportation, restaurant lunches, and work clothing, some home businesses can be the ideal income generator for a single-parent family. You have to be suited for a home business if you are going to succeed. Here are a few thoughts for you to consider.

Tips for Starting a Business

- Give your business a name, and have business cards printed.

- Design and distribute a flyer that explains your service. Here are some tips for creating an effective flyer:

    Use a memorable or provocative headline, and choose words such as "easy," "now you can," "proven," etc. If you already have a satisfied customer, ask the person to write an endorsement of your service or product. A large image is more impressionable than a series of smaller ones. Use borders, shadings, contrasting colors, etc; and if you're on a tight budget, use bright-colored paper and black ink. Bold your titles and subtitles, but avoid using all capital letters. Consid offering a coupon or a limited-time discounted price. Be sure to verify phone numbers and Web sites on your flyer, and ask someone else to proofread it—another set of eyes is helpful![69]

- Get a partner, if needed.

- For pricing information, call similar services in your area and ask what they charge.

Getting Started

- Consider how much it would cost to set up your business and how much you can invest.

- If starting a new business, learn all you can about the business from the library or others in the business.

- Check local zoning, tax, and legal regulations for small businesses.

- Contact the Small Business Administration for information.[70] They have an abundance of information on the Internet but will also mail you a resource guide if you request one.

- Start small; keep your expenses low.

- Spread the word with business cards and flyers and through friends and relatives.

A WORD OF CAUTION

There is no shortage of advertised "opportunities" for making a lot of money from home in a hurry, but beware of these, since often they are scams.

Many of these ads neglect to mention how many hours you'll be expected to work without getting paid. Many of these schemes require that you purchase your own envelopes, paper, postage, or other supplies, as well as place newspaper ads at your expense and pay for photocopying.

You might be dazzled by an envelope-stuffing offer that promises big bucks. You can even picture yourself relaxing at home and spending quality time with your children while you work. Unfortunately, in reality, you'll most likely have to put up a fee for the privilege, and you'll find out that the promoter never had any employment to offer you. Your fee might be spent on a letter from the advertiser telling you to place the same envelope-stuffing ad in newspapers or magazines.

Another program requires you to invest in equipment or supplies to do assembly or craft work. But once you've made the aprons or baby shoes or plastic signs, the company tells you your work didn't meet their standards and they won't pay you. Unfortunately, none of your work will ever meet their standards, and you're stuck with the equipment, loss of money and time, and dozens of aprons. (Well, look on the bright side—aprons make nice gifts. . . .)

If you think you're working with a legitimate work-from-home business, get answers to these questions in writing:

What tasks will I have to perform? (Ask the program sponsor to list every step of the job.)

Will I be paid a salary, or will my pay be based on commission?

Who will pay me?

When will I get my first paycheck?

What is the total cost of the work-at-home program, including supplies, equipment, and membership fees? What will I get for my money?[71]

And remember that in most cases, an offer is not legitimate if you have to send money up front to get started.

 *Jade, a single mother of seven-year-old Andy, says, "There are plenty of ways of maintaining a reasonable lifestyle without the high cost of doing it. Learn to find those ways by asking around, taking a chance, asking God to show you how, and you'll be surprised what you'll come up with! I had a college education and worked outside the home but felt a huge burden to spend more time with my child. I found out through friends that the local school was in*

need of teachers and that the local college had a fast-track program for teaching certificates. Within months I was enjoying many more days off with my son at virtually the same pay. There was also a mandatory retirement plan, which I had been putting off "getting around to" for some time!

CHAPTER 9

Reflecting God's Image

God, Money, the Church, and You

"Everyone at your church is so happy," Merry said wistfully. She continued explaining her observation to her friend Melanie. "I wish my family was like the ones I see at your church."

"What do you mean?" Melanie asked.

"Couples. Married couples with two point five children. Great houses. Plenty of money. You know."

"Actually, if you got to know the people in our church better, you'd have a little different picture," Melanie replied, smiling. "We all have stuff to deal with. We just do our best to deal with it together!"

"How do you know?" Merry asked.

"See Dan over there?" Melanie pointed discreetly. "His wife left him and the kids and went off with an old boyfriend. He's raising three girls by himself. And Debbie's husband died suddenly; now she's alone with two teenage boys. And there's Abby; she has a three-year-old and she never married the father. We're not picture-perfect here."

"Wow," Merry said. "Maybe I could fit in here better than I thought!"

You might have said to yourself, *If only I were married, my finances would be in a lot better shape.* Maybe. But married couples also have financial struggles, and couples argue about money more than about any other subject.

You might be disappointed that at this point in your life you're raising children by yourself—or you may be in a great season of life! You are not a single parent *only*. You might also be a son or daughter, a sister or brother, an employee, a church member, a Christian, a bowler, a volunteer, a neighbor . . . and you are a mother or a father.

And wherever you are in life and however you came to the point you're at, remember that there is no one typical situation or ideal family. One parent says, "My family is different. But most families these days are different, and so that makes us about average, I guess. . . . I don't think of [our home] as broken. The family stretched and cracked and, like glass, had to be sent back to the fire and reblown. It's in a different shape now than the one I originally planned. But it's in good shape and it works. Families these days come in all shapes."[72]

It is when we have needs that we experience the grace of God more fully. No one wants to go through the process of having less-than-ideal circumstances, but later, we're glad to have the results of these times.

A person who has had an easy road in life will not have as much wisdom to give to others. "Praise be to the . . . God of all comfort," Paul says in 2 Corinthians 1:3–4, "who comforts us in all our troubles, so that we can comfort those in any trouble with the comfort we ourselves have received from God."

"The LORD is close to the brokenhearted and saves those who are crushed in spirit" (Psalm 34:18). Would you be as close to the Lord as you are today if you had never been brokenhearted?

"Consider it pure joy, my brothers and sisters, whenever you face trials of many kinds" (James 1:2 TNIV). This perhaps is one of the most difficult spiritual truths to embrace. Why does James say this? Because "the testing of your faith develops perseverance. Perseverance must finish its work so that you may be mature and complete, not lacking anything" (1:3–4). It's the end result that's important.

And what does all this have to do with money? As already mentioned, there are more than 2,350 references to money in the Bible. The Lord knows that money is a big part of our lives. He warns us against loving money, but He also wants us to be good managers of what He has given us.

For many people, talking about God and money reminds them of the health-and-wealth false teaching that has tripped up many. But it's a fair point to wonder about: Does God really care about money?

We've journeyed through this book on the belief that He does. We know He has promised to meet our needs. We believe that what He gives us He asks us to manage well—to give from what we have, to save but not hoard, to plan for the future, and to spend wisely.

How does the church respond to people who need help? Christians respond to the whole person, not just the immediate need for a greater cash flow—although sometimes that will be appropriate. But a philosophy that attempts to solve problems with money does not take into consideration the whole needs of the family. The biblical church does not respond to people with one-size-fits-all solutions, but looks at the individual as precious, as made by God, as someone whose name God knows and whose very hairs on the head are counted. Christians are committed to sticking with a family, not just putting a bandage or a short-term solution on a problem, but growing with that family as its members grow more and more like Christ.

For many decades, some Americans have looked to the government to provide solutions to situations that ideally would be handled by families and churches. If you are currently receiving benefits, you most likely feel stuck in a holding pattern even though you'd like to move on. It may seem like a long road to independence apart from government aid,

YOU CAN **BANK** ON IT

Since we are not meant to walk through life alone, part of being a good manager is getting help when we need it. The church is God's hands and feet to bring that help.

but I encourage you not to give up! Keep your eyes on your goal to be self-supporting with God's help.

Pray for your specific needs. God has promised to be a husband to the husbandless and a father to the fatherless (see Psalm 68:5 and Isaiah 54:5). You can be honest with Him about your needs.

Ask your family for help. "If anyone does not provide for his relatives, and especially for his immediate family, he has denied the faith and is worse than an unbeliever" (1 Timothy 5:8). These are strong words, but they show that God's plan is for families to care for one another. You may not have parents or other family members who can help you, and the extended family of a former spouse may or may not be an option when you need help—but if possible, don't discount these sources of help.

You should be part of a local church body of committed Christians. The church, as we mentioned, is God's way of meeting the needs of the body. Some churches, it is true, have been taken advantage of by needy people who feel entitled to get what they can. Show the church that this is not your intention. Get involved. Find ministries for which you are gifted, and put your talents to work in the church. Be part of social activities that are for people of all ages and stations in life. Don't compartmentalize yourself as "the single parent." Be Scott or Polly or whoever you are!

Many Christians have found it helpful to have a prayer partner and/or an accountability partner. Find one person with whom you can be open about your situation and your needs, and ask that person to hold you accountable. Perhaps you have trouble sticking to your spending plan; perhaps you're tempted to give in to an impulse purchase that you shouldn't make. Call your accountability partner. You'll be surprised to learn that your struggles are universal! And you won't just be the recipient of strength and encouragement—you'll also be an encourager.

"The real measure of your wealth is how much you'd be worth if you lost all your money."[73]

If part of your plan to financial freedom is to work with a coach, continue to do so and take his or her counsel.

- God will use money to build up our trust in Him. Jesus reminded His followers, "Do not worry, saying, 'What shall we eat?' or 'What shall we drink?' or 'What shall we wear?' For the pagans run after all these things, and your heavenly Father knows that you need them. But seek first his kingdom and his righteousness, and all these things will be given to you as well" (Matthew 6:31–33). Sometimes it's easier to trust God for the big things we don't have any control over than for our everyday needs.

- God will use money to develop our trustworthiness. So much of our lives revolve around making money, spending money, saving money, and giving money. God measures our ability to handle spiritual riches by our stewardship of material wealth.

  "Whoever can be trusted with very little can also be trusted with much, and whoever is dishonest with very little will also be dishonest with much. So if you have not been trustworthy in handling worldly wealth, who will trust you with true riches?" (Luke 16:10–11).

- He provides what we need: "And my God will meet all your needs according to his glorious riches in Christ Jesus" (Philippians 4:19).

  And He provides joyfully: "Which of you, if his son asks for bread, will give him a stone? Or if he asks for a fish, will give him a snake? If you, then, though you are evil, know how to give good gifts to your children, how much more will your Father in heaven give good gifts to those who ask him!" (Matthew 7:9–11).

- As God provides in small things, our confidence in His care begins to grow; and the more our confidence in Him grows, the more He will supply. "For the Scripture says, 'Whoever believes in Him will not be disappointed.' For there is no distinction between Jew and Greek; for the same Lord is Lord of all, abounding in riches for all who call upon Him" (Romans 10:11–12 NASB).

- God will use money to unite Christians through sharing blessings. "He who gathered much did not have too much, and he who gathered little did not have too little" (2 Corinthians 8:15). God will use the abundance of one Christian to supply the needs of another.

"Money will buy you a pretty good dog, but it won't buy the wag of his tail."[74]

At another time He may reverse the relationship, as described in 2 Corinthians 8:14: "At the present time your plenty will supply what [others] need, so that in turn their plenty will supply what you need." It is important, as we face times of economic challenge, that Christians accept the principle that a surplus of money in our lives, indeed, everything we have, is there for a purpose.

- God will use the abundance or lack of money to provide direction for our lives. Too often we believe God will direct our lives only through abundance of money, and we keep probing to see where He supplies it. However, God can steer us along His path through the lack of money just as quickly. "I have learned to be content whatever the circumstances. I know what it is to be in need, and I know what it is to have plenty. I have learned the secret of being content in any and every situation, whether well fed or hungry, whether living in plenty or in want" (Philippians 4:11–12).

- God can use money to satisfy the needs of others. Christians who hoard money and never plan for their financial lives cannot experience this area of fulfillment. Often I hear Christians say, "How can I give? I barely have enough to meet my needs now." If we have never learned to give, we are missing out on God's generous provision. "Give, and it will be given to you. A good measure, pressed down, shaken together and running over, will be poured into your lap. For with the measure you use, it will be measured to you" (Luke 6:38).

SINGLE PARENTS AND THE LOCAL CHURCH

Single parents' needs are often invisible in the church. More and more families have needs, but the church will not know about them if you are not open about them. And if you are open about your own needs, you may well be an encouragement to someone else who also has needs.

The sales principle of "the law of 200" says that at any given moment, each of us has at least two hundred people in our circle of influence. If this is true, you can assume that at least one person—and probably more—is struggling with some great need.

Single parents, like anyone else, need to be surrounded with ongoing spiritual and emotional support. This support provides them with a sense of community and connection. And churches that provide these things find their membership and financial support actually increase, because believers who join them strengthen these efforts. (See the resource section in this book for practical helps for churches working with single parents.)

> People always say, "I could never do what you do. I don't know how you do it." Like carrying a two-year-old and a five-year-old who is half of my weight. Or juggle full-time school, work, and kids. Sometimes I wonder how I do it. But I have become accustomed to my routine, and with God's help, we keep going and it doesn't seem like too much.

Here are some ways to encourage single parents and their children:

- Drop a note or card in the mail. It's fun to open the mailbox and find something other than bills and junk!

- Write a note to the child(ren). Children love to get mail! Include their very own Arch Card or certificate for another treat.

- Babysit so the single parent can have a break. If your own children are old enough, enlist their help. Younger children love to be with teenagers! Or take children with you on an outing.

- Invite a single-parent family to your home for meals. While offering hospitality to them during the holidays is wonderful and much appreciated, single parents need meals, caring, and fellowship throughout the year.

- Offer to coach youth sports. Whether you are the coach or a parent with a child on the team, invite a child from a single-parent family to be on the team, and offer to transport the child to practices and games if possible.

- If you are good with cars, offer to change the oil and fix minor automotive problems.

- Take a single parent shopping at a shopping warehouse and split the cost and quantity in bulk purchases. And it's not only single parents who need to save money on groceries and other items!

- Sometimes a single parent is just tired out. Think how you can help the family have fun—take them to the roller skating rink, order a pizza to be delivered, invite them over for movie night.

- When you make a meal that can be frozen and reheated, make more than your family needs—let your single-parent friend have a pot of chili for the freezer. Lasagna, spaghetti sauce, sloppy joes, all freeze well. (Remember, we're talking about food you're making today, not yesterday's leftovers!)

- Listen. Sometimes just a sympathetic ear is what is needed.

Be sure your friend knows you will keep the details of what he or she is sharing confidential.

- Do you have clothing you can give to the single parent? Many people need to dress up at least to some extent at work, and anything new is appreciated.

- How about an inexpensive or one-time-use camera and a certificate for having film developed? Or offer to use your video camera to film the family's special occasion.

- Pick up some new games the family can play together— *Uno, Crazy Eights*, and many others are fun and not so time-consuming that the working parent will be overwhelmed with even more to do.

- A school supply store is a great place to find some unique items such as unusual card games and sturdy wooden puzzles.

- Sort through toys and books in good condition and offer them to a single-parent family.

- Let a single parent plan a movie night. Find out what movie the family would like to see and drop it off along with plenty of popcorn. You might even plan to stay and watch the movie with them, since the family would appreciate company and the chance to be hospitable.

- It's a pleasure to be thought of. Small kindnesses like flowers from your garden, a homemade dessert, or an encouraging phone call can go a long way.

- Most of all, take the initiative to offer your friendship. With all the rigors of work and the responsibilities of home and family, many single parents don't have the time to nurture and develop relationships they need with other adults. Go first. Call and offer kind words of love and encouragement. Get together for coffee or an ice cream cone. It could be the start of a wonderful new friendship that will last for a lifetime.

- Ask your church to keep a record of people in the congregation who have abilities in different areas and who would be willing to donate their services for free or for a low cost when needed —electricians, mechanics, plumbers, and so on offer vital services, but many times a single parent just can't afford to call one from the phone book.

- Give single parents a gift subscription to a Christian magazine. Focus on the Family, for example, has a variety of magazines for children of all ages, teenagers too, as well as excellent resources for single parents. Call 1-800-A-FAMILY.

- Offer childcare free or at low cost for single parents who work; or team up with others to help out. Irene found herself raising two daughters alone and needed childcare for them while she worked. Four women in her church helped out—each took the girls for a week at a time.

- If the church has someone knowledgeable about finances, ask that person to be a resource to people—single and married—who need counsel. For those families who can't afford it, the church could pay a stipend.

- As mentioned previously, a church wide clothing exchange can be arranged. This won't be only for single parents, but for everyone. Have a variety of people on the team to plan this event.

- Start a mentoring program or a support group for single parents. A loving, trusted mentor or a couple who befriends the single parent and his or her children can be a lifesaver, especially during the first year as a single parent, which could be the most traumatic.

- Children from single-parent families need exposure to families and parent role models missing from their own family. Positive role models can change children's lives. They need men and women who are willing to participate in their lives—as teachers, scout troop or youth group leaders, sports coaches, and so on.

- Christian men, especially, are needed to be good role models for boys.

- Simply having an adult notice and take a minute to talk with and show interest in a child means a lot. This focused attention is important for both girls and boys.

- Include single parents in adult activities and seasonal celebrations at the church. People can offer to provide transportation or help with childcare (or childcare costs) so single parents can attend church events and fellowship events.

- Be sure your church offers activities for all adults; not all singles—parents or not—want to always be with other singles and be compartmentalized in this role.

- Can you offer to help with children after school? Often the hours between school and supper are the busiest and most tiring. Can you help children with homework or studying even once a week?

- Men and women and teens can help single parents with mowing and yard jobs, washing cars, washing windows, and babysitting.

- Although no one needs to be someone's "project," remember single-parent families when the youth group is making service calls on older members to perform such chores as mowing the grass, weeding, washing cars. A working parent doesn't really get a day off, and Saturday can go by quickly with errands and chores to do.

- Churches need to make the members aware of the loneliness single parents can experience during the holidays and on weekends. "I remember when Heidi and I first moved to a new area and didn't have anyone to share Sunday dinner with," said one single parent. Holidays or other special occasions can also be difficult.

These are just a few ways you can encourage the church to help single parents and make a significant difference in their emotional, spiritual, and physical health. As one of God's children and part of His church, I want to encourage you. As you seek to apply His financial principles, I know that you will be encouraged by His love and faithfulness as you see the results. We have seen many times over that a person who puts these principles into practice will draw closer to God. I pray that happens for you. I pray that you and your children will find a place of worship that is an encouragement to you and where you can be a witness to others.

The little girl asked, "Would you rather have times or things"—good times to remember or things to keep, like bank accounts, homes of our own, and such things?

Things alone are very unsatisfying. Happiness is not to be found in money or in houses or lands, not even in modern kitchens or a late model motor car. Such things add to our happiness only because of the pleasant times they bring us.

But times would be bad without some things. We cannot enjoy ourselves if we are worried over how we shall pay our bills or the taxes or buy what the children need.

And so we must mix our times and things, but let's mix 'em with brains, as the famous artist said he mixed his paints, using good judgment in the amount we take.

LAURA INGALLS WILDER
JULY 1922[75]

Godliness with contentment is great gain (1 Timothy 6:6).

The Envelope, Please

Keeping Track of the Money

"Let's see," Kevin muttered. "I know I had a twenty yesterday. . . "

He scrounged around in his pockets, blew dust off the Altoid and ate it, found a five-dollar bill and three ones, and a Canadian nickel.

"Let me think." Kevin had stopped at the video store on his way home yesterday and paid the late fee. Then he had gone to . . . um . . . yes, he'd bought some cat food . . . but he should still have more than eight dollars left. Where had it gone?

No wonder the kids are always losing things was the unbidden thought that came to him.

Briefly Kevin wished he were still married so he could put the responsibility on someone else to take care of this. But there was no one else, just him. He needed to learn to keep better records.

Now that you've made out at least a rough spending plan—or you haven't yet, but you're still reading, so you have good intentions—it's time to go over some ways to keep track of where your money is going.

Kevin could have easily pulled out his notebook and checked where that money had gone if he had gotten into the habit of jotting down even small expenses. It was still hit-and-miss for him, but he was trying!

As mentioned previously, it's a good idea to keep track of cash spent, even for miscellaneous items such as coffee or a newspaper. This isn't to convince you never to spend money on these things, but to let you see written out where that dollar went. If you haven't gotten in the habit of doing this, invest in a small notebook you can keep in a pocket or purse, and begin. You'll want to start with recording $.85 for the notebook!

Some people feel that keeping track of expense and spending is too complicated, so they discard it. Or after a couple of setbacks, they give up.

Since you're not going to give up, we'll start with the most basic and simplest way of keeping track of where the money should go—the envelope system.

The Envelope, Please

Someone quipped that the envelope system is Grandma's cookie jar—when the jar is empty, there's no more money to spend.

Create an envelope for each category of bills you pay—housing, insurance, food, utilities, gasoline, clothing, and so forth.

Either imagine a stack of money or go ahead and cash your paycheck. Put the amount of money you need for each category in its envelope.

It's easy with this system to see where your money is and where it must go—there it is, right in front of you, in green and white.

You'll take money out of the utility envelope when the phone bill is due; you'll go into the grocery envelope when you run out of milk; and when your teenage son announces one evening that he needs white gloves to march with his high school band *tomorrow*, you'll find enough money in the clothing envelope (which might be easier than finding white gloves).

When the money allocated for one category—for instance, for recreation or entertainment—is gone, you'll have to wait until next payday to have more funds for that category.

Since you most likely won't be keeping actual cash in your home, you can use a partial envelope system. Then you'll write checks to pay your bills or have the money directly transferred from your checking account to pay bills electronically. You can still use a simple envelope system by keeping cash available for areas that are harder to budget, such as gotta-have-a-pizza night, which is entertainment . . . or for son Rick's white gloves for band.

Jenny has a sticky note in the monthly planner she keeps in her purse. She writes down her fixed expenses for the month and on the planner writes the days they're due. When the month is over, she moves the note to the page for the next month and begins again.

Other Systems

Grandma's cookie jar really isn't a bad system. But today there are many tools available to you to help you keep track of where your money should go and where it went.

Crown Financial Ministries offers a wealth of information and products to help you. Visit their Web site, or phone 1-800-722-1976. Crown has an envelope-system product to make tracking your spending plan easy, and also has a software version called Mvelopes.

Crown also has forms available for you to record your expenses and payments by categories and explains how you can transfer surplus from one category to your savings. An important worksheet they offer that you might want to review is the Income Allocation Sheet. This is where you decide how much you're putting aside from each paycheck for each expense area to guarantee that you'll have the funds when needed.

You can also get individual help in working out your spending plan with a Money Map coach at no charge from Crown Financial. E-mail mmcoaching@crown.org.

Willow Creek Community Church offers free online forms to help you track expenses, as well as other financial resources. Go to www.willowcreek.org and find Ministry Quick-Link. Scroll down to Good Sense and go to Resources.

You can keep one of these forms on your kitchen counter or other easily accessible place. Each day you'll record what you've spent in groceries, gas, clothing, and so on, and you'll mark off the date so you know you've completed your record for that day. Of course, you won't be spending something each day in every category.

Good Sense offers another form for your fixed expenses such as housing and insurance.

Reconciling Your Checkbook

If you use a hard copy of your bank statement to reconcile your checkbook, you'll find the instructions to do so on the back of your statement. You can also reconcile your checking account electronically. One benefit of the Internet is that you can check your bank balance daily if you like. You'll probably not need to use this service every day, but keeping up on your checkbook balance at least weekly is a good idea. You can see what checks have been cashed and keep your account up to date accurately.

Make a check mark next to each entry that has already been cashed. Take the balance shown and subtract all other checks you have written but that are still outstanding—that is, they have not yet been cashed but will be.

Now you know what your bank declares is in your account. If there is a major difference in what you show and what the bank shows, contact their customer service department and straighten it out as soon as you can.

Keep in mind that yesterday's transaction might not appear on this morning's statement. For example, if you went to the bank yesterday at four o'clock and cashed a $50 check, that amount might not yet show up as a debit on the next day's statement. Be sure to account for that money and subtract it from the balance your statement is showing.

Many of us carry debit cards and use these instead of checks for everyday purchases. This is fine, but *don't forget to record the deduction in your checkbook!* Keep a receipt or notation and make the entry in your checkbook as soon as you can.

Likewise, a deposit you made yesterday will be on record, but might not show up on your statement today. Check your account again tomorrow.

You can, of course, also reconcile your account monthly when the statement comes in the mail to you from the bank.

If you keep a ledger besides the one in your checkbook, reconcile your records with the bank statement. Again, if there is a significant difference, contact the bank.

- Separate your cash into categories.

- Allot an amount for each category. If you're paid more than once a month, divide your monthly expenses up so you'll have enough when the bill is due.

- If you use up all the money in one category, don't spend any more until you have another payday.

- If you often forget to write your checks in the ledger, get checks that duplicate, or copy, what you're writing. These are a little more expensive, but less costly than bouncing forgotten checks.

- Keep ATM and debit receipts and write these deductions in the checkbook as soon as you can.

- Reconcile your bank statement as often as you need to but *at least* once per month.

- Remember to record automatic deductions from your checkbook ledger. The money will be taken from your account whether or not you remember to write it in. The bank will remember.

- Use a system that works for you. Don't overcomplicate it!

- And whether you use a pen and paper, or software, or a combination of both—

  Write it down!

SPENDING PLAN WORKSHEET
Income, expenses, suggested percentage guidelines

■ **TOTAL MONTHLY INCOME:**

_____

Less giving_____

Less taxes_____

Less savings_____

■ **SPENDABLE INCOME:**

_____

■ **HOUSING: 25–35%**

Mortgage/rent _____

Insurance_____

Utilities _____

Telephone _____

Maintenance _____

■ **AUTO: 12–15%**

Car payment _____

Auto insurance_____

Gas, oil _____

Maintenance _____

License, etc._____

■ **HOUSEHOLD: 10–15%**

Groceries _____

Cosmetics _____

Cleaning _____

■ **CLOTHING: 5–6%**

_____

■ **INSURANCE: 3%**

Medical _____

Dental _____

Life _____

Other_____

■ **DEBTS: 5%**

Credit cards_____

Education _____

Bank _____

Other_____

_____

■ **MISCELLANEOUS: 5–8%**

Cell phones _____

Eating out _____

Sports/lessons _____

School supplies _____

School lunch _____

Allowances _____

Gifts_____

Vacation _____

Other medical _____

■ **CHILDCARE: 0–5%**

Day care _____

Tuition_____

Other_____

DEBT REDUCTION PLAN
List of debts

	Creditor	Total Due	Minimum Monthly Payment	Extra Monthly Payment
1.				
2.				
3.				
4.				
5.				
6.				
7.				
8.				
9.				
10.				

Arrange your list in order: greatest balances and highest interest rates to least. Make your minimum monthly payments on all, adding at least $5.00 to it if possible. Concentrate on completely paying off the smallest balances and the balances with the highest interest rates first. When one account is paid off, roll the amount you've been paying on that one into the next smallest account.

Record of Debts

Creditor	Total Due	Minimum Monthly Payment	Extra Monthly Payment
Credit card			
Credit card			
Credit card			
Dentist			
School loan			
Bank loan			
Personal loan			
Other			
Other			
Other			

IMPORTANT RECORDS
and where to find them

DOCUMENT	LOCATION
■ Birth certificates	_____
■ Vehicle registrations	_____
■ Vehicle titles	_____
■ Insurance information	_____
■ Bank information	_____
Account numbers	_____
Type of account	_____
Safe-deposit boxes	_____
■ Will	_____
■ Social Security numbers	_____
	_____
■ Marriage license	_____
■ Divorce decree	_____
■ Passport	_____
■ Other	_____
	_____

FOR KIDS: *Tracking where money goes*

In the boxes below, fill in where you have spent money each day. For example, your boxes might be labeled giving, saving, school lunch, clothes, snacks, DVD rental, and so on. You'll have a lot of blanks on this sheet because you won't be spending money in every category each day. You may copy this form so you'll have a new one each month.

Month of _____

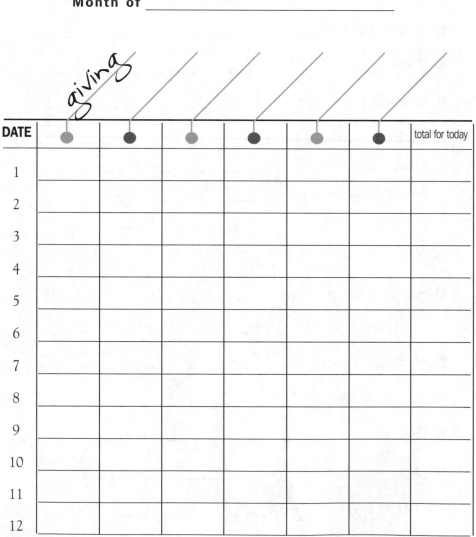

DATE	giving						total for today
1							
2							
3							
4							
5							
6							
7							
8							
9							
10							
11							
12							

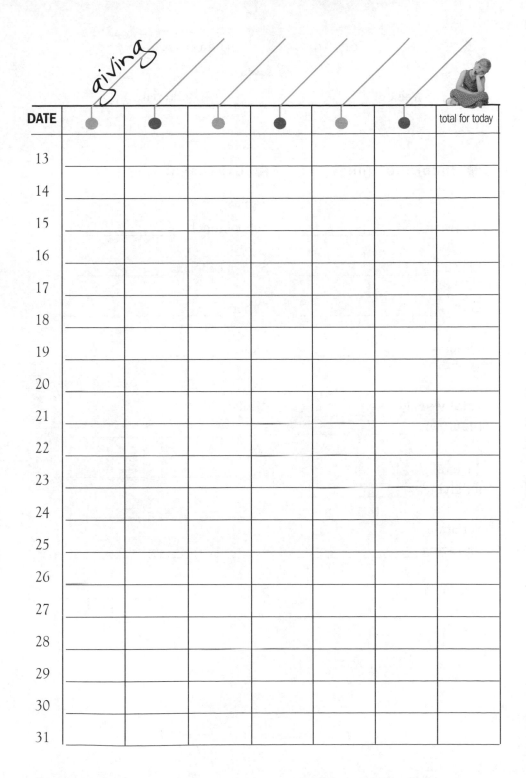

DATE	giving						total for today
13							
14							
15							
16							
17							
18							
19							
20							
21							
22							
23							
24							
25							
26							
27							
28							
29							
30							
31							

FOR KIDS:  and expenses

Week of_____(add dates)

● **INCOMING MONEY:**   ● **EXPENSES:**

Needs:

Allowance: _____   School lunch:_____

Extra: _____   School supplies: _____

Gifts: _____   Other: _____

Other: _____   Other: _____

Total weekly   *Wants:*

income: _____   1. _____

Take off   2. _____
for giving:_____
                                3. _____
Set aside
for saving:_____   4. _____

Available   5. _____
money: _____

Acknowledgments

Thanks to my assistant, Karen Kubacki, who has been with me now for over ten years. She helped keep me in balance and kept our work going while I concentrated on this project. She not only held down the fort but gave great insight on the book.

Thanks to my family, who saw little of me at times while working on this book, for their support—especially my single-parent daughter and grandson who live with me.

Thanks to my dear friends and associates who gave greatly appreciated input and opinions as we worked through some areas of the book.

And thanks to the following for adding their expertise: Elizabeth Brown, Christian Real Estate Network, Del Coon, Scott Gibson, Bob Henderson, Karen LeCompte, Nancy Sebastian Meyer, Tim Miller, Ed Santiago, Luci Tehan, Terry Westerhoff.

Resources

TAX INFORMATION:
- www.irs.gov; 1-800-829-1040 or check your directory for the phone number of your local IRS office.

ORGANIZATIONS:
- Crown Financial Ministries—phone 1-800-722-1976 or visit www.crown.org.
- Contact the Good Sense Ministry at Willow Creek Community Church at 1-847-765-5000 or visit willowcreck.org.
- Financial Peace (Dave Ramsey): www.daveramsey.com
- Focus on the Family—phone 1-800-A-FAMILY or visit www.family.org.

CAREER:
- Personality evaluations:

  DISC (www.inhisgraceinc.com)
  www.advisorteam.org

Books:

- There are many books about money management written from a biblical perspective. Check with your church library or your local Christian bookstore.

For Churches:

- Brenda Armstrong and Mercy Tree Ministries offer several resources for churches in their work with single parents.

- Visit the Web site at the link below or phone 770-831-9418 for information about:

Single Parent Ministry Training Manual
More Than Babysitting—Ministering through Childcare
Empowering Single Parents—Ministering through Welfare-to-Work
Fixing Cars to Fixing Lives—Ministering through Car Care
Reaching the Heart of the Home—Ministering through Housing

http://www.mercytree.org/mercytree/index.cfm?fuseaction=
content.home&grp=3&sub=67

NOTES:

1. Lee Jenkins, *Taking Care of Business: Establishing a Financial Legacy for the African American Family* (Chicago: Moody, 2001), 19.

2. Carol Lynn Pearson, *One on the Seesaw: The Ups and Downs of a Single-Parent Family* (New York: Random House, 1988), 101.

3. Cynthia Yates, *Living Well as a Single Mom: A Practical Guide to Managing Your Money, Your Kids, and Your Personal Life* (Eugene, OR: Harvest, 2006), 63.

4. Deborah Taylor-Hough, *Frugal Living for Dummies* (New York: Wiley, 2003), 24.

5. Ron Kittle in www.quotegarden.com/money.html.

6. Jenkins, *Taking Care of Business*, 74.

7. Ibid.,75–76.

8. Ibid., 75.

9. Larry Burkett with Randy Southern, *The World's Easiest Guide to Finances* (Chicago: Northfield, 2000), 33.

10. You can find forms at willowcreek.org/GoodSense/resources.asp. You can also go to www.crown.org, click on Tools, and use the Online Budget Guide.

11. Crown Financial Ministries offers budget counseling. Call 1-800-722-1976 for a Money Map coach, or go to www.crown.org. Dave Ramsey's organization also offers budget counseling. Go to www.daveramsey.com/fpu/counsel ing/ for more information.

12. Jenkins, *Taking Care of Business*, 152.

13. Dave Ramsey, "Too Broke to Tithe?" http://www.christianitytoday.com/tc/2006/001/8.24.html.

14. Jenkins, *Taking Care of Business*, 156.

15. The IRS sponsors VITA, the Volunteer Income Tax Assistance Program. This program offers free tax help to low- to moderate-income people. VITA sites are usually located at libraries, schools, malls, churches, and other locations. Call 1-800-820-1040 for a location close to you.

16. http://www.insurance.com/Article.aspx/Financial_Tips_for_Single_Parents/artid/195.

17. www.irs.gov/publications/p590/ch05.html.

18. www.ed.gov/inits/hope/.

19. From a *Washington Post* word contest, quoted in quotegarden.com/money.html.

20. Mary Sarton, www.quotegarden.com/home.html.

21. Kin Hubbard, www.quotegarden.com/housework.html.

22. Habitat for Humanity has built houses for thousands of families since its founding in 1976. Go to www.habitat.org for information on this Christian-based organization.

23. http://www.thedesertsun.com/apps/pbcs.dll/section?Category=topics01.

24. http://financialplan.about.com/cs/cars/a/SaveGas.htm.

25. www1.eere.energy.gov/consumer/tips/driving.html.

26. http://financialplan.about.com/cs/cars/a/SaveGas.htm.

27. http://www.thedesertsun.com/apps/pbcs.dll/section?Category=topics01.

28. Author unknown, www.quotegarden.com/money.html.

29. http://www.ftc.gov/bcp/conline/pubs/autos/usedcar.htm.

30. Mac MacCleary, www.quotegarden.com/driving.html.

31. Suze Orman, "Ten Ways to Drive Down Your Car Costs," http://finance.yahoo.com/columnist/article/moneymatters/4177?p=1.

32. Deborah Taylor-Hough, *Frugal Living for Dummies.*

33. Ibid.

34. Angel Food is one such program. Anyone can participate, regardless of income. You can buy one box of food per month, usually for $25—a $50 or more value—that is preplanned and changes from month to month. Visit www.angelfoodministries.com for more information and to see if there is a location near you that sponsors this ministry. Another similar program found in several midwestern states is Heartland Share. You can visit their Web site at www.heartlandshare.com.

35. *Mad* magazine, quoted in www.quotegarden.com/money.html.

36. American proverb, www.quotegarden.com/debt.html.

37. Howard Dayton, *Free and Clear: God's Roadmap to Debt-Free Living* (Chicago: Moody, 2006), 97.

38. David F. Woods, "Single Parents: The Necessity of Life Insurance," http://www.parentswithoutpartners.org/vaWoods.htm.

39. Walter Updegrave, "Ask the Expert," http://money.cnn.com/2002/12/17/pf/expert/ask_expert/.

40. http://www.insurance.com/Article.aspx/Financial_Tips_for_Single_Parents/artid/195.

41. http://www.ssa.gov/dibplan/dqualify.htm.

42. The Christian Brotherhood Newsletter is a Christian organization whose philosophy is that Christians should take care of other Christians. This alternative for health insurance (it is not an insurance company or plan) might or might not be right for you. Be sure you investigate what your obligations are and what the organization takes care of. Your monthly gift to this ministry entitles you to certain payment of some medical costs; they try to keep your monthly payment low enough so that your spending plan will keep enough in it for doctor visits for routine checkups, vaccinations, and so on. For more information, visit www.christianbrotherhood.org, or phone 1-800-791-6225.

43. www.MsMoney.com/mm/planning/marriage/college_planning.html.

44. Attributed to both Andy McIntyre and Derek Bok, www.quotegarden.com/education.htm.

45. NOTE: fafsa.com is a site not affiliated with the U.S. government, but they will apply for you for a fee.

46. Deborah Taylor-Hough, *Frugal Living for Dummies*, 112.

47. Ibid., 114.

48. June Solnit Sale and Kit Kollenberg with Ellen Melinkoff, *The Working Parents Handbook* (New York: Simon & Schuster, 1996), 280–81.

49. http://home.ivillage.com/decorating/budget/0,,14c4-2,00.html.

50. Deborah Taylor-Hough, *Frugal Living for Dummies*, 97.

51. http://www.stretcher.com/stories/04/04aug16h.cfm.

52. Deborah Taylor-Hough, *Frugal Living for Dummies*, 101.

53. Krisi Davis, *The Sea Glass Hunter: Living a Productive Life as a Christian Single Parent* (Baltimore: PublishAmerica, 2006), 48.

54. KidsNCommon is one such site, especially for divorced parents. See www.kidsncommon.com.

55. Alexandre Dumas fils, *Camille*, 1852, quoted in quotegarden.com/money.html.

56. Krisi Davis, *The Sea Glass Hunter*, 46.

57. Dave Ramsey, "The Spiritual Aspect of Money," *Relevant*, Issue 21, July–August 2006.

58. Carol Lynn Pearson, *One on the Seesaw*, 105.

59. Stephen R. Covey, *The 7 Habits of Highly Effective People: Powerful Lessons in Personal Change* (New York: Fireside, 1989), 108.

60. Ibid., 106–107.

61. Randall Hansen, copyright by Quintessential Careers. The original article can be found at http://www.quintcareers.com/creating_personal_mission_statements.html. Reprinted with permission.

62. Ibid.

63. Dennis Bakke, *Joy at Work* (Seattle: PVG, 2005), 248.

64. Ibid., 247–48.

65. George Horace Lormier, quoted in quotegarden.com/money.html.

66. Dennis Bakke, *Joy at Work*, 247–248

67. Created by Nancy Sebastian Meyer for *Financial Relief for Single Parents*.

68. www.businessknowhow.com/startup+12ways.htm.

69. Karen Saunders, www.macgraphics.net, "10 Easy Ways to Make Your Flyer Stand Out in the Crowd," © 2006. Used with permission.

70. www.sba.gov; click on FAQS, go to Starting Your Business: or go directly to http://app1.sba.gov/faqs/faqindex.cfm?areaID=1.

71. www.ftc.gov/bcp/conline/pubs/invest/homewrk.htm.

72. Carol Lynn Pearson, *One on the Seesaw*, xii.

73. Author unknown, quoted in quotegarden.com/money.html.

74. Henry Wheeler Shaw, quoted in quotegarden.com/money.html.

75. Laura Ingalls Wilder, "Times and Things," July 1922, *Little House in the Ozarks, A Laura Ingalls Wilder Sampler: The Rediscovered Writings*, edited by Stephen W. Hines (Nashville: Thomas Nelson, 1991), 154.

Larry Burkett's *World's Easiest Guide to Finances*

It's easy to get into debt, it's easy to put off planning for your retirement, and it's easy to live without a detailed budget. Perhaps this is all so easy because it is nearly impossible to figure it all out at once.

Larry Burkett and Randy Southern have put together a feasible and comprehensive guide that everyone can understand. And suddenly it becomes *easy* to put your finances back together.

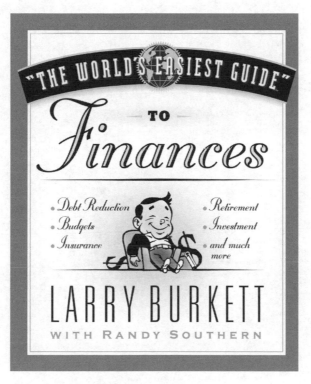

ISBN: 1-881273-38-5
ISBN-13: 978-1-8812-7338-7

America's Family Financial Expert

In *1/2 Price Living*, Ellie Kay outlines the workable possibility of a family being able to live on just one income. This fun and easy-to-read book gives practical steps, creative suggestions, and valuable resources to help you and your family cut your expenses in half and have fun in the process.

ISBN: 0-8024-3432-0
ISBN-13: 978-0-8024-3432-6